INTRODUCTION TO INDUSTRIAL LAW

By

J. B. CRONIN, LL.B.

Reader in Law at the University of Southampton

and

R. P. GRIME, B.A., B.C.L.

Senior Lecturer in Law at the University of Southampton

LONDON

BUTTERWORTHS

1974

ENGLAND:	BUTTERWORTH & CO. (PUBLISHERS) LTD.
	LONDON: 88 KINGSWAY, WC2B 6AB
AUSTRALIA:	BUTTERWORTHS PTY. LTD.
	SYDNEY: 586 PACIFIC HIGHWAY, CHATSWOOD, NSW 2067
	MELBOURNE: 343 LITTLE COLLINS STREET, 3000
	BRISBANE: 240 QUEEN STREET, 4000
CANADA:	BUTTERWORTH & CO. (CANADA) LTD.
	TORONTO: 14 CURITY AVENUE, 374
NEW ZEALAND:	BUTTERWORTHS OF NEW ZEALAND LTD.
	WELLINGTON: 26/28 WARING TAYLOR STREET, 1
SOUTH AFRICA:	BUTTERWORTH & CO. (SOUTH AFRICA) (PTY.) LTD.
	DURBAN: 152–154 GALE STREET

ISBN—casebound: 0 406 56940 1
limp: 0 406 56941 X

Made and printed in Great Britain by
Butler & Tanner Ltd., Frome and London

Preface

Industrial law, or labour law, can be studied in a variety of different ways. It can be a vehicle for a sociological examination of law; it has a fascinating history; it presents innumerable problems of conceptual analysis and interpretation. Academics in the field sometimes forget that there are many people whose primary interest in their subject is practical: people who work with or alongside the law of employment, industrial relations and industrial accidents. It is at such persons, whether in training or practice, that this book is primarily aimed.

It would, of course, be both misleading and absurd to imply that an interest in the practicalities of law necessarily excludes all concern with other approaches to the subject. The law has to be understood, and it usually cannot be understood save by reference to its social context, its history or its concepts. This is not intended to be a book of rules: in particular, we have not thought it desirable to over-burden the text with detailed quotations from the statutes. Readers of this book will find that, at appropriate places, the Industrial Relations Act, the Code of Practice on Industrial Relations, the Factories Act, the Redundancy Payments Act, etc., will have to be referred to and read in conjunction with it.

We hope that this book fills a gap. It seems to us that there is a need for a concise introduction to the whole field of industrial law which is neither too detailed or academic to be of use to those whose interest is immediate and practical, nor too dry to be either interesting or truly informative. We feel that those who study industrial or labour law otherwise than in the course of a law degree might find a use for it, as might those who practise in the field of industrial law, most of whom, of course, would not primarily describe themselves as lawyers.

January 1974   John Cronin
                                                       Robert Grime

Contents

Contents

Contents

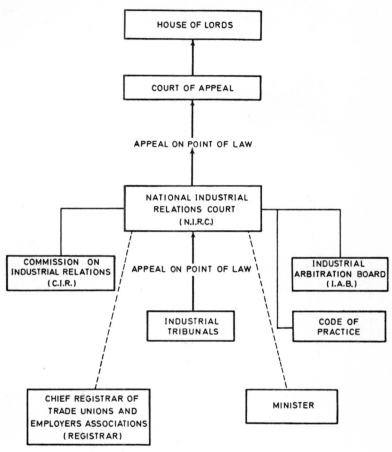

Fig 1

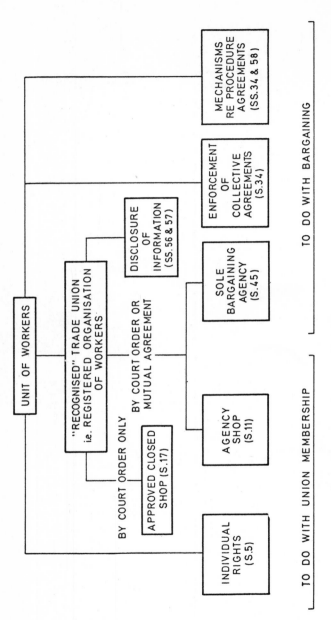

UNIT OF WORKERS

"RECOGNISED" TRADE UNION i.e. REGISTERED ORGANISATION OF WORKERS

BY COURT ORDER ONLY

BY COURT ORDER OR MUTUAL AGREEMENT

DISCLOSURE OF INFORMATION (SS. 56 & 57)

APPROVED CLOSED SHOP (S.17)

INDIVIDUAL RIGHTS (S.5)

AGENCY SHOP (S.11)

SOLE BARGAINING AGENCY (S.45)

ENFORCEMENT OF COLLECTIVE AGREEMENTS (S.34)

MECHANISMS RE PROCEDURE AGREEMENTS (SS.34 & 58)

TO DO WITH UNION MEMBERSHIP

TO DO WITH BARGAINING

ALL THESE "MECHANISMS" ARE PROTECTED BY THE CONCEPT OF UNFAIR INDUSTRIAL PRACTICE

Fig 2

Chapter 1

The Industrial Relations Act
Its Organs and Structure

The political uproar over the Industrial Relations Act 1971 almost totally obscures the fact that it is an elaborate attempt to change the whole structure of industrial relations and is therefore as much concerned with industrial peace as with industrial war. It is inevitable that it has a great effect upon a variety of aspects of industrial law: these effects are described in the appropriate section of this book. But the Act also sets up new organs and structures which are complex and important enough to need a chapter to themselves.

I ORGANS

The organs of the Act are shown diagrammatically in Fig. 1, but additional commentary is needed:

The National Industrial Relations Court (NIRC)

Figure 1 shows that NIRC is at the centre of the web of organs operating the Act. It is a division of the High Court and a unique one. Although its President is a professional judge and either he or some other such judge takes part in every hearing, there must also be not less than two lay-judges (*i.e.* non-lawyers) sitting as well. In theory, therefore, NIRC is controlled, or controllable, by non-lawyers. How far in fact the non-lawyer members of the Court do exercise their independence is not (and never likely to be) known. But the lay-judges

3

are in no sense assessors or assistants: they are judges of the High Court.

The Act requires that lay-judges be drawn from parts of the community skilled in industrial relations. At the time of writing the boycott of the Court by the trade union movement is still in operation and the composition of the Court is therefore seriously unbalanced.

In keeping with its revolutionary composition, the *modus operandi* of the Court is exceptional. There are no formal pleadings and proceedings are begun by an application on a simple *pro-forma*; the rules of evidence do not apply; and any person, legally qualified or not, may appear on behalf of a party to a case. The Court's rules of procedure also give it a wide discretion to join other parties it considers relevant to the issues before it. Costs are not awarded (save in rare cases in order to punish frivolous proceedings). It sits at odd hours. The aim is that NIRC should be a simple, cheap and speedy court.

It is hard to see why it was thought necessary that there should be an appeal from NIRC but, as Fig. 1 shows, there is, to the Court of Appeal on a point of law, and thence to the House of Lords. As interpretation of the meaning of a statute is always a point of law, this means that the authoritative interpretation of the words of the Industrial Relations Act will be given not by NIRC but by the ordinary courts that are superior to it.

The Commission on Industrial Relations (CIR)

The CIR existed before the Act as a standing Royal Commission which investigated matters of general industrial relations interest. This function continues: it examines industrial relations questions referred to it by the Minister (s. 121) and reports back (s. 122). It also issues an annual report on industrial relations, in which it may draw the Minister's attention to particular problems (s. 123).

The CIR is now a statutory body under the Act. It consists of not less than six and not more than fifteen Commissioners appointed by the Minister. Its new function is to act as the investigating arm of NIRC. Repeatedly in the Act, where applications are made to NIRC, the Court is required to refer the matter to the CIR for investigation. Examples are s. 11(3) (agency shop) and s. 46(1) (sole bargaining agency). In no case is the CIR given power to make decisions. That is the prerogative of NIRC. But clearly the reports and investigations of the CIR must have great influence.

The Industrial Arbitration Board (IAB)

The Industrial Courts Act 1919 established a standing Industrial Court to arbitrate in industrial disputes. Its importance might be gauged by the paucity of people who knew that it existed. In order to avoid possible confusion with NIRC, the Act renames it the IAB. It has only two new functions under the Act. First, if an employer has failed to negotiate in good faith with a sole bargaining agent, NIRC may permit a claim to be presented by the union in question to the IAB for settlement (s. 105(5)). Secondly, a similar claim may be allowed in case of non-disclosure by employers of information required by s. 56 of the Act (s. 102).

Industrial Tribunals (ITs)

These tribunals were set up to resolve problems arising out of the Industrial Training Act 1964. They have legally qualified chairmen and, originally, a representative of workers and a representative of employers. The trade union boycott of the Industrial Relations Act has meant that the two lists have had to be reconstituted as one list of "persons skilled in industrial relations" and that there has been a serious shortage of workers' representatives. The Redundancy Payments Act 1965 gave further jurisdiction to the tribunals (see p. 41) and their work has been very greatly increased by the Industrial Relations Act. Their main new functions relate to unfair dismissal (see p. 47) and breaches of the entrenched rights given to employees under s. 5 of the Act (see p. 77). Appeal on a point of law lies to NIRC and thence upwards.

Like NIRC, the tribunals operate a vastly simplified procedure compared with, say, the Magistrates' Courts. The rules of evidence do not apply, simple forms are used instead of pleadings, and any person can appear on behalf of an applicant or respondent. Lawyers are not encouraged.

The Chief Registrar of Trade Unions and Employers' Associations (The Registrar)

The process and results of registration under the Act are dealt with at p. 68. The Registrar is an independent, quasi-judicial official appointed by the Crown and holding office during Her Majesty's pleasure: but he is closely related to NIRC and is in truth part of the organic structure of the Act. Thus, he has a great deal of discretion, but many of his decisions are subject to an appeal to NIRC. He may, on occasion, initiate proceedings in NIRC (see, for instance, s. 76: application to NIRC in respect of "defective" trade union rules).

The Minister

It may seem a little strange to include the Secretary of State for Employment in the judicial and quasi-judicial organs of the Act, but he has two potentially important organic functions under the Act. First (s. 58), he can make far-reaching applications to NIRC in respect of procedure agreements: even to the extent of asking NIRC to impose such an agreement where none exists (see p. 96). Secondly, it is he who initiates the emergency procedures (s. 138 *et seq.*; see p. 118).

Code of Practice

Like the Minister, the Code of Practice hovers uneasily between the organs and the structures of the Act. The Code is approved by Parliament (on strictly party lines) and prepared by the Department of Employment. Its stated aim is "to give practical guidance for promoting good industrial relations". Its significance lies in s. 4 of the Act which requires that NIRC and the tribunals take the Code "into account" where it is "relevant" to any question before them. Presumably it is for them to say whether it is relevant or not. Comparison of the relative precision of parts of the Code with the broad statements of the Act leads to the conclusion that, in the long run, the Code will have considerable influence on the Act's interpretation. Compare, for instance, s. 22 of the Act, which sets

out the law on unfair dismissal, with paras. 120–133 of the
Code, which deal in much greater detail with the same matters.

II STRUCTURES

The shape of the Act is hard to grasp at first. This is
because, for ideological reasons, it starts with a statement of
aims and then goes on to give to workers certain entrenched
rights with regard to joining or not joining a trade union.
From here it is logical to proceed to other problems of trade
union membership such as the closed shop.

In fact the real starting point of the Act is a series of definitions in s. 44, and Fig. 2 is an attempt to show diagrammatically how the whole conceptual architecture of the Act
stems from the idea of a "unit of workers". This term is
not used in any section of the Act, which is why it is used
here. Instead there are various other phrases, *e.g.* "bargaining
unit" (s. 44); "one or more descriptions of workers" (s. 11);
"unit of employment" (s. 37); "undertaking" (s. 57). All have
slightly different technical meanings but, in practice, they all
relate back to the concept of a unit of workers. They are each
dealt with in the appropriate section of this book; the purpose
of this passage is to describe their interrelationship as a whole.

Thus, each worker in a unit of workers is given the right,
by s. 5, to belong or not to belong to a trade union. This
means, of course, the end of the traditional closed shop. In
its place, the Act offers the Agency Shop or, much more rarely,
the Approved Closed Shop. But Fig. 2 shows that these
options are open only to a *registered* trade union; an unregistered union has no equivalent way of protecting and increasing
its membership under the Act.

The figure also shows that unregistered unions suffer disabilities in the field of collective bargaining. Only a registered
union can become a compulsory Sole Bargaining Agent or will
have the legal right to the disclosure of information required
by s. 57 when it comes into effect.

III   SANCTIONS

The draftsman of the Act has protected its structure by the invention of a new form of sanction: the "unfair industrial practice". It is not a crime nor a tort, it is something *sui generis*. It means that if someone fails to comply with an obligation laid on him by the Act, an aggrieved party may go either to NIRC or to a Tribunal, whichever is appropriate, and claim a declaration of rights, compensation and, sometimes, a "desist" order. Compensation is the most important of these remedies by a long way. The amount will vary according to the status of the person against whom the award is made. The compensation that can be awarded against an employer (save in the case of unfair dismissal, for which see p. 47), an employee or an unregistered union is limited only by the value of the damage caused. Compensation against a registered union is restricted to maxima based on the number of its members.

It should be remembered that, because NIRC is a part of the High Court, failure to pay compensation it awards or disobedience of an order it issues can amount to contempt of court and so lead to fines or imprisonment. But there is virtually no *direct* use of the criminal law in the Act.

Chapter 2

Employment

I WHAT IS EMPLOYMENT?

Industrial law is essentially the law that applies to employment and to those who are employed. The first question, then, must be: "who is employed?". In a broad sense, this is easy to answer. Everyone who works for someone else can be said to be employed. The weekly wage-earner at a factory, the odd-job man who mends a broken window for a householder, the teacher, the company director, the policeman, the consultant surgeon, the judge, all work for others and are all employed. But they clearly differ and it is often important in law to distinguish between them. Acts of Parliament, for example, contain precise definition clauses which state exactly to which categories of employee they are to apply.

Lawyers, then, usually find they cannot answer this simple first question except with another: "employed for the purposes of what?". For a person who is "employed" for the purposes of the rule of law which makes an employer liable to pay damages to those injured by the wrongful acts of his employees, may not be "employed" for the purposes of the National Insurance Acts, and he may not, therefore, be entitled to sickness benefit. It is only when the precise legal context is known that it becomes possible to give an answer.

However, there is one very large category of employee which is so important that, for many purposes, it is possible to regard it as "the" definition of employee. This is the employee who is employed to work under the orders of his employer (either generally, or within a specific area). He is called in law, by the rather old-fashioned name of "servant". Most employees are servants: how they carry out their work

9

is subject to the control of their employers. The biggest class of employees who are not servants are "independent contractors": men who—like the odd-job man mentioned in the first paragraph—are not subject to their employer's control as to *how* they work but are simply paid to produce results. If I engage a taxi to take me to the station, the driver is an independent contractor: if I have a chauffeur, he is my servant.

This is the easiest way to define servants—in terms of control. But it will not do in all cases:

> Mersey Docks and Harbour Board owned cranes which it hired to various firms of stevedores. The cranes were manned by drivers appointed by the harbour board and paid by them but who were inevitably working on behalf of the stevedores and subject to their general direction. The question arose as to whether a crane driver ought to be considered the servant of a firm of stevedores or of the harbour board. His evidence, that "he took no orders from anyone" was accepted as true by the court. Nevertheless, the House of Lords held that he remained the servant of the harbour board. They appointed him, paid him and had the right to dismiss him: they therefore must be taken to have the *right* to give him orders, despite the fact that they never exercised that right.
>
> *Mersey Docks and Harbour Board* v. *Coggins and Griffiths* (1947) HL

By similar reasoning, it is not difficult to hold that hospital medical staff are the servants of the hospital authorities, and that the latter are therefore liable for the negligence of the former (*Cassidy* v. *Minister of Health* (1951) CA; *Roe* v. *Minister of Health* (1954) CA). But it is not very clear when such a *right* to give orders might exist. Some judges spoke of a man being a servant when he was "part and parcel of the organisation" of his employer (*Stevenson, Jordan and Harrison Ltd.* v. *Macdonald and Evans* (1952) CA). Most cases are easy: it is only the rare marginal case that causes problems. Recently the approach of the courts has been to weigh all the facts to see which way, in the end, the balance tips. So in one case:

> A firm of concrete manufacturers made contracts with each of their drivers under which he took his lorry on a hire purchase contract and became responsible for its maintenance and running costs. He was paid in accordance with the concrete he delivered, but minimum annual earnings were guaranteed. He was obliged to comply with the directions of competent staff and to wear the company's uniform. The judge examined all the facts and decided that the driver's position was, in the end, "consistent with that of a servant", and held him to be one.

Ready Mixed Concrete (South East) Ltd. v. *Minister of Pensions* (1968) QB

Most of industrial law is concerned with servants, but other categories are sometimes relevant. Apart from independent contractors, which we have mentioned, there are public officers, such as judges or police officers, who have a legally recognised *public* status, and are therefore not subject to all the rules relating to servants. There are crown servants, both civil and military, whose employment is very like that of a servant, but subject to the overriding rights of government in some respects. There are those whose employment is service coupled with some other status, such as a registered dock worker, who has rights under the dock labour scheme, or a trade union official, or a managing director of a company, who have a position under the rules of the union or the articles of the company respectively. Above all, it is important always to remember that the question "who is employed?" can only be answered with the question "employed for the purposes of what?"

II   THE CONTRACT OF EMPLOYMENT

Every employee has a contract of employment. Occasionally, it is a formal written agreement, but usually it is an informal affair to be gathered from conversations, letters, notices, advertisements and the like. All that is necessary for a legally binding contract is that there should be an agreement of the sort recognised by the law. In general the law recognises as contracts all agreements for lawful purposes where each party gives something in return for what he gets. So a simple offer of work in return for wages, when accepted, constitutes a contract.

It is common to speak of contracts being "enforced", but that can be misleading. If one party fails in his contractual obligations, it is only rarely possible to get a court to order him to carry the contract out. Such orders are never available for contracts of employment (see the Industrial Relations Act 1971, s. 128, which enacts an older rule of law: *Britain* v. *Rossiter* (1882) CA). The primary legal remedy is damages—a remedy whose value depends in part upon the ability of the other party to pay.

But breach of contract may be important in other ways. If the breach is a serious one—if it "goes to the root of the contract" and seriously affects the possibility of future performance—then the other party is legally entitled to bring the contract to an end. This idea is clearly important in contracts of employment in connection with dismissal. Again, it is sometimes possible to apply to the court for an order not that a contract shall be performed but that a specific part of it shall not be broken. These negative orders (called injunctions) are not issued if the practical effect is to force performance (see the Industrial Relations Act 1971, s.128(1)(*b*), and *Warner Bros, Pictures, Inc.* v. *Nelson* (1937) QB) and are only met in connection with breach of a specific term, not in respect of failure to perform the whole contract. So they may be issued to prevent an employee setting up in competition with his employer, in breach of his contract, or, occasionally, to prevent an employer issuing an invalid notice of termination (*Hill* v. *C. A. Parsons Ltd.* (1971) CA). Finally, a breach of contract may be a factor in other legal questions—such as whether a strike constitutes a tort, (a civil wrong giving rise to a claim for damages by those injured).

Whatever the practical consequences when a contract is broken, the contract of employment provides the primary source of the legal obligations of the employer and the employee. These obligations are found in what are called the *terms* of the contract. In theory, a contract is an agreement and its terms are what have actually been agreed by the parties when the contract was made. The obvious practical difficulty is proof. We can never really discover what lies in people's minds: it is certainly unreliable to ask them afterwards what they thought they intended. In real life we have to be content with drawing reasonable inferences from what they said and did. So we can find the terms of a contract of employment in what was said when the man was taken on, in written documents such as advertisements, notices and handbooks that were used at the time, and in letters that passed between the parties.

With regard to documents and letters, however, an important distinction has to be made. By a rule of convenience, the law presumes that a man has read what he signs, so every part of a document signed as part of a contract becomes a term of that contract. This can be hard:

> A café-owner bought a cigarette machine by instalments. She signed a long, almost illegible, contract without reading it. One of the many clauses deprived her of her right to sue if the machine was faulty. She was held to be bound by the clause.
>
> *L'Estrange* v. *F. Graucob Ltd.* (1934) CA

There is no such rule for unsigned documents. Here a man is bound by the contents only if it is reasonable to expect him to have read them. What is reasonable will depend upon a lot of things—the nature of a document, its clarity, its prominence or availability, and so on. One cannot be dogmatic, but in many employment situations there are established ways of making terms of employment known—slips in wage packets, "official" notices, works rule-books and the like —and it can generally be assumed that these will provide sources of contractual terms.

Most contracts are made once for all: if I make a hire purchase contract today, it is the terms of that contract and nothing else which will govern me for the next two years. A line is drawn at the moment of agreement.

> Some property belonging to a guest was stolen from a hotel room. A notice in the bedroom clearly stated that it was a term of the contract with the hotel that the hotel should not be legally liable for such a loss. But this was held to be ineffective. It could not have been brought to the attention of the guest until *after* the contract had been made.

> *Olley* v. *Marlborough Court Ltd.* (1949) CA

This is not easy to apply to a continuing relationship like employment. In the nature of things, conditions of work change over the years. Wages and methods of working change, employees are assigned to other work or promoted. But these changes cannot have any *legal* significance until it can be said that there is a contractual basis for them which means, in practice, until it can be said that the change has been understood and adopted by agreement of both parties. The agreement is, in strict theory, an agreement to abandon the existing contract and to replace it with a new one which incorporates the proposed new term. Usually, of course, all that one has to go on is the fact that a change was introduced and, perhaps, acted upon. It is rare to have any more direct evidence of the agreement of employer and employee on the matter and, therefore, as always, one is driven back to inference. The extent to which it is legitimate to infer agreement from the absence of overt opposition in the context of employment can be almost infinitely arguable:

> An employee who had been suspended by his employers on disciplinary grounds brought an action to test the validity of the suspension. The only available evidence was that he had been employed for many years in the same factory and that his employers had used the penalty of suspension during that period without complaint from him or from any other employee. The Court of Appeal, by a majority, held that the suspension was lawful.

> *Marshall* v. *English Electric Co.* (1945) CA

The case neatly illustrates the difficulties. For one judge, no question of acceptance of the right to suspend arose. There was evidence to support the inference that Marshall had agreed to it when he took the job. The others disagreed, but one was prepared to hold that his continuing to work for a long period in knowledge of the practice of suspension had eventually matured into full contractual acceptance, although it was not possible to be precise about when this happened. The third judge was simply not satisfied that Marshall and the other employees had ever accepted suspension as a legal right of their employers, pointing out that men who could be dismissed at very short notice might accept suspension *as a fact* "lest a worse fate befall them". Where the employee *does* exhibit overt opposition, however, the position is clearer:

> In order to carry out an agreement reached with a trade union, an employer gave his non-union employees written notice of a change in the terms of their employment and required them to join the union. Eventually the plaintiff, who had refused, was given notice of dismissal "for breach of contract". The whole operation had lasted for more than a year, but the plaintiff had refused to comply with the proposed change at every stage. It was held that he had no legal obligation to join the trade union.

Hill v. *C. A. Parsons, Ltd.* (1971) CA

In these questions the law is almost excessively concerned with the individual. The contract is between an individual employee and his employer and it is his individual agreement that is at issue. But, as always, it is only the exceptional case that causes problems.

Since 1963 employers have been under an obligation, imposed by the Contracts of Employment Act, to issue to employees, within 13 weeks of their starting work, written particulars of some of the more important terms of their contracts of employment. The particulars must be kept up to date: employees must be notified of changes within a month. Strictly, of course, these documents are not themselves terms of the contract, merely notice of terms. They may be inaccurate, and if they are, the employee may go to an Industrial Tribunal to have the document rectified. But once it has been issued and accepted without complaint, it will inevitably constitute powerful evidence of what the terms really were (see *Camden Exhibition* v. *Lynott* (1966) CA). The present Act (1972) covers the following matters:

> Date of commencement of the employment.
> Name of the parties.
> Rate and method of calculating pay.
> Pay interval—weekly, monthly, etc.
> Working hours, or normal working hours.
> Holiday entitlement and holiday pay (if none, the fact must be stated).
> Sick-pay (if none, the fact must be stated).
> Pensions (if none, the fact must be stated).
> If the employment is for a fixed term, the date of expiry.
> Length of notice of termination for both parties.
> In addition the notice must contain: a note of the employee's rights in respect of trade union membership and activities under s. 5 of the Industrial Relations Act 1971; details of any grievance procedure available to him; and the name of the person to whom he must apply if he has any complaint although all these matters are not necessarily part of the terms of his contract.

The Act permits the employer to discharge his obligations either by issuing a document containing all this information, or by issuing a "reference document" directing the employee to reasonably accessible documents containing the information. Reference documents may also indicate that the "accessible documents" will contain notice of any relevant changes and so relieve the employer of the administrative responsibilities of informing all employees individually of all changes.

III COLLECTIVE AGREEMENTS

In practice many of the terms of employment of most workers are settled by collective bargaining. It is only the law, with its long tradition of individual contracts, that insists upon regarding employment as something bargained between individuals. Collective agreements raise two quite separate legal questions: first, their effect upon the legal obligations of those who negotiate them—trade unions and employers or federations; secondly, their effect upon the contracts of employment of the workers for whom they are made. The first question will be dealt with in Chapter 7. All we need say here is that it has no bearing at all upon the second question. Whether or not a collective agreement is legally binding it will have exactly the same effect upon the workers' contracts of employment.

Applying the general principles discussed above, a collective agreement becomes part of the individual contract of employment when it is incorporated by agreement. There are, of course, those who are employed expressly on the terms of collective agreements. In other cases, no doubt, continued work in the knowledge of collectively agreed terms will usually serve to bring the terms of the collective agreement into the contract of employment. It is also fair to say that the courts have shown themselves very willing to find evidence that collective agreements have become part of the contracts of employment and therefore have become legally enforceable by and against individual employees:

> A colliery deputy was taken on by a contract which provided that it should be subject to "national and county agreements . . . for the time being in force". Three years later his union made a new agreement which the defendant worked under for some years, but which he later rejected. The court held that he had broken his contract of employment by this rejection. The subsequent agreement had become a term of that contract both by the fact of his working under it and by his original agreement to be bound by such documents.

N.C.B. v. *Galley* (1958) CA

A pay increase was negotiated between a trade union and an employer but before it was possible to pay it the government called upon both sides of industry to observe a wage standstill. It was held that nevertheless the wage increase had been incorporated into the contract of employment of the plaintiff, so that he had a legal right to it.

Allen v. *Thorn Electrical* (1968) CA

Sometimes (but rarely) a union will act on behalf of a specific group of members, or workers, in such a way as to make it, in law, their agent. In such cases the individuals concerned will obtain an immediate right, for it is *their* contract made through the union as "conduit pipe". But this is unusual: unions more commonly act more generally and independently. (See *Edwards* v. *Skyways* (1964) QB—severance payments negotiated for redundant pilots.)

Occasionally the law steps into this rather confused arena and specifically enacts that a collective agreement shall have contractual effect as between employer and employee. The Terms and Conditions of Employment Act 1959 preserves a remnant of the system of compulsory arbitration of industrial disputes which existed during and after the second world war. Under s. 8 of this Act (as amended by the Industrial Relations Act 1971), where terms and conditions of employment are established in an industry or area by agreement or award a union (provided it is registered under the Industrial Relations Act) may make a "claim" to the Minister that a particular employer is not observing those conditions. The matter is referred to the Industrial Arbitration Board and, unless the employer can show that he is observing terms that are "not less favourable", an order will be made. The effect of an order is, among other things, to incorporate into the contracts of employment of the workers concerned a term entitling them to the established conditions.

The Industrial Relations Act, perhaps surprisingly in view of the importance it attaches to the question of the legal enforceability of collective agreements as such, has little to say on their incorporation into contracts of employment. Section 147, which deals with strike notice, merely assumes that incorporation may occur, expressly or impliedly.

IV   IMPLIED TERMS

So far we have covered the legal inferences which may be drawn from what is said and done by employers and employees. But in employment, as elsewhere, a very great deal often goes without saying. A man may be taken on on the sketchiest of terms—perhaps wages, hours of work and a general description of duties will be mentioned, but nothing else. Where does the rest come from? Much will come from the sort of process which, in law, went on in the case of *Marshall* v. *English Electric*, mentioned earlier. A man will start work, observe the conditions that are in practice observed, and at some stage be taken to have agreed to them by the fact of his continuing work without complaint. In this way, the "custom and practice" of the workplace may become contractually binding. But this legal process is supplemented by two others.

First, there is what is known as a *"term implied in fact"*. A contract is an agreement and its terms are usually derived from what was said and done by the parties at the time. If agreement can be inferred from words and actions, why not from silence and inaction, if, in the circumstances, there are some things which are so obvious to both parties that one would not expect comment? If A is a chimney-sweeper by trade and B asks him to sweep his chimneys, then A will be entitled to the rate for the job even though nothing was said about money: it is obvious to everyone that a professional chimney-sweep only works for money. As one judge put it:

"Prima facie that which in any contract is left to be implied and need not be expressed is something so obvious that it goes without saying; so that if, while the parties were making their bargain, an officious bystander were to suggest some express provision for it in their agreement, they would testily suppress him with a

common 'Oh, of course'." (*Per* MacKinnon, L.J., *Shirlaw*
v. *Southern Foundries (1926) Ltd.* (1939) CA)

In employment this is not always easy to apply. The crucial
word is "common". The tacit understanding and agreement
has to be common to both parties:

> An employer sued his employee in respect of damages
> the employer had had to pay because of the employee's
> carelessness in doing his work, driving a lorry. In his
> defence, the employee pleaded an implied term that he
> should be able to take advantage of the insurance policy
> taken out by the employer in respect of the vehicle he
> drove. The defence failed partly because it was not poss-
> ible to say with any precision what exactly employer and
> employee might have agreed to in the matter: the sug-
> gested term was far too vague.

Lister v. *Romford Ice and Cold Storage Ltd.* (1956) HL

> A man left his trade union, without clearing the arrears
> of his subscriptions, and joined a rival organisation. In
> subsequent proceedings before the Disputes Committee
> of the T.U.C., under the T.U.C.'s Bridlington Agreement,
> the second union was directed to expel him as having
> been admitted in contravention of that Agreement. There
> was no term in the contract of membership (the rule-
> book) permitting expulsion for this reason, but the union
> claimed that there was an implied term. The argument
> failed, as the plaintiff had never heard of the Bridlington
> Agreement when he had joined.

Spring v. *NASDS.* (1956) Lanc Pal Ct

Secondly, there are *"terms implied in law"*. Over the years,
the courts have developed certain presumptions with regard
to contracts of employment (and certain other contracts).
These presumptions will take effect as implied terms in the
contract, unless the parties modify them by their own express
agreement. These terms are not so much precise rules as

general principles. Sometimes they overlap and there is some fuzziness at the edges. But the central cases, which are the more common, should be clear:

(*a*) The main duty of the employee is to serve his employer. Service means he must be ready to work when called upon and thus gives to the employer the right to give orders within the general scope of the employment contracted for. Of course, there are limits to this power to give orders. An employee need not obey orders that are illegal (*Gregory* v. *Ford* (1951) QB—employee not obliged to drive uninsured lorry), or which involve his running real risks of personal danger (see *Bouzourou* v. *Ottoman Bank* (1930) HL; *Ottoman Bank* v. *Chakarian* (1930) HL, two cases involving unsettled conditions in Turkey showing that while an employee might be ordered to run *general* risks he might not be ordered to run a *specific* identifiable risk), or which are outside the ambit of his employment (see *Royle* v. *Dredging and Construction Ltd.* (1966) IT—a lorry-driver could not be put to general labouring unless he agreed). Within such limits, the employer may give such orders as he thinks fit, subject to any special arrangements (with regard to chains of command, for example) as may have been made as part of the contract of employment.

An employee who fails to serve—to work in accordance with his employer's orders—breaks his contract. But it is not by failing to *work* that he breaks it: it is only when he fails to *serve*. If, for example, he is unable to work for reasons beyond his control—sickness, for example—he commits no breach of contract. He is ready and willing to work, although temporarily unable. Furthermore, unless such illness or other inability amounts to a really serious disablement such as is likely to prevent him from ever working in that capacity again, the interruption will not of itself destroy the contract. Employment is usually an indefinite contract and, viewed against the possible duration of a working lifetime, even relatively long-term illness amounts only to a temporary interruption.

If, as we said, the main obligation of the employee was to serve—to be ready and willing to work to the orders of his employer—then that is what his employer buys with the wages he promises to pay. The bargain is wages for service. It follows, then, that, in principle, an employer is under no obligation to provide work for his employees to do. "Provided I pay my cook her wages regularly, she cannot complain if I take any or all of my meals out" was how one judge expressed it (Asquith, J., in *Collier* v. *Sunday Referee* (1940) KB). Of course, this may be modified by the contract, including any term implied from the practice of the employment in question. Employees who are paid by commission, wholly or in part, or those paid on piece-work systems, could easily show that their employer commits a breach of contract if he simply refuses to give them work to do (*Devonald* v. *Rosser* (1906) CA). But employees paid simply by reference to time cannot complain if they are given nothing to do, although they can claim their wages until their contracts are properly terminated by valid dismissal.

The same principles can be applied to sickness. A sick employee remains employed until his contract is validly terminated. So long as he remains employed, provided that he is not paid under a piece-work system or any other method that depends on actual work done, he is entitled to his wages.

> A shop assistant was taken ill with rheumatism and was off work for nearly four months. On his return, he was given a week's pay and dismissed. He sued and was awarded four months' wages.
>
> *Marrison* v. *Bell* (1939) CA

Like the obligation to provide work, this can be modified by the contract. Since in practice the majority of workers do not get paid in full during sickness, the legal question is whether that practice has become a term of the contract. A sick-pay scheme contained in a notice on the works notice-board (*Petrie* v. *Mac Fisheries Ltd.* (1940) KB) and previous acceptance of a "no work, no wages" rule (*O'Grady* v. *M. Saper Ltd* (1940) CA) have both been held sufficient to deprive an employee of his right to wages during sickness.

(*b*) Employment is also a relationship of mutual trust, care and confidence. Both employer and employee must take reasonable care to look after each other's interests. Thus an employer must take care for the safety of his employees and at one time it was usual to express this as a matter of contract. Today, however, it is treated as a question of tort, and is dealt with in this book in a later chapter under "Employers' Liability". For his part, the employee must take care not to damage his employer—though in modern times this is not usually a question of causing personal injuries. It is much more likely to be a matter of causing economic loss by damaging property or otherwise.

> Father and son were employed by the same employer. The son, a lorry-driver, while manoeuvring his vehicle in the factory yard, struck and injured his father. Father sued the employer, who, under the principle of vicarious liability, was responsible for the negligence of his employees, and recovered substantial damages. The employer's insurance company, as they were entitled to do under the policy, sued the son in the name of the employer, for breach of contract. They succeeded. An employee commits a breach of contract if through his negligence he causes his employer loss.

Lister v. *Romford Ice and Cold Storage Ltd.* (1957) HL

But the obligations go further than this. An employee must not act against the commercial interests of his employer. He must respect his trade secrets and his customers; he must respect the confidentiality of any confidential information entrusted to him.

> A milk roundsman attempted to solicit his employer's customers to transfer their business to him when he set up by himself, as he intended to. This was a breach of contract.

Wessex Dairies v. *Smith* (1935) CA

> A carter, on his way home from work, injured a boy who was trying to interfere with his employer's property. It

was held that he had a legal duty to do so, and that, therefore, his employer was responsible.

Poland v. *John Parr* 1927) CA

A sales manager left his employment and took with him details of a price-ring which he sent to the Daily Mail. The Court of Appeal held that, although such action was in general a breach of contract, in this case, since the price-ring was illegal, the employers could have no remedy.

Initial Services v. *Putterhill* (1968) CA

Five employees of a manufacturer of miniature radio valves worked in their spare time, for "expenses", for a rival. There were no trade secrets involved and the market was large enough for both manufacturers. But the employees were breaking their contracts simply by working for a rival.

Hivac Ltd. v. *Park Royal Scientific Instruments Ltd.* (1946) CA

To put it very shortly: an employee must look after his employer's interests.

(c) An employee acts on behalf of his employer and, subject to anything in the contract, his employer must not only provide him with the means to do his job, but indemnify him for any expenses or losses incurred in so acting. For his part, the employee must hand over all the profits or products of his work to his employer. This means that his employer is entitled to everything that the employment produces, but to no more. This is well illustrated by inventions. If a research chemist discovers a new substance it is his employer who may patent it and exploit it. It came from the employment. On the other hand, if a van-driver, working for the same employer, invents a device to make his vehicle run more economically, that invention is his and does not belong to the employer. Of course, the situation may be expressly regulated by contract, and there is nothing to prevent the employer either buying inventions from employees or granting them some share in inventions that in law belong to him. But the basic principle is: what comes from the employment belongs to the employer, what comes from elsewhere belongs to the employee. And it is of no consequence where or when the work is done—the research chemist may make his discovery on Sunday afternoon at home, the van-driver may develop his device in his employer's workshop in his employer's time—the principle holds. The line is difficult to draw, especially in cases where the "product" of the employment is not tangible. After all, as one judge put it, "the defendant has gained much skill and aptitude and general technical knowledge . . . but such things have become part of himself, and he cannot be restrained from taking them away and using them".

> A film actor was given the name "Stewart Rome" by his studio, and became famous. Later he parted company with his studio and they attempted to prevent his using the name. But the court held that the name was his—it had become valuable because of the exercise of his own skill and because of his personality, not just because of his employment.
>
> *Hepworth Manufacturing Co.* v. *Ryott* (1920) Ch D

Although the Patents Act 1949, the Copyright Act 1956 and the Registered Designs Act 1949 contain provisions relating to inventions etc., by employees, the central principle is not affected and is, of course, much wider. *All* products of the employment outside the employee's personal skills, even when they are neither patentable inventions, registrable designs or works to which copyright attaches, belong to the employer. An excellent example of such "property" is "know-how".

The final point which can be made in this connection is that the employee must hand over to his employer *all* profits of the employment.

> The owner of a fishing fleet sold out to a larger company and took a position as an employee of that company. However, he continued to receive bonuses from an ice

company in respect of ice used by "his" boats, since he
was a shareholder of the ice company. He was held
obliged to account for the bonuses to his employer.

Boston Deep Sea Fishing Co. v. *Ansell* (1888) CA

The principle is wide—it has been held to cover profits made
by an army sergeant from using his uniform to assist
smugglers in Egypt (*Reading* v. *A-G* (1951) HL). It would
cover tips and similar gratuities, although in such cases there
would usually be an express or implied term permitting the
employee to keep them.

There are other rules developed in the last century which
have very little practical relevance today. An employer of
domestic servants, for example, used to be obliged to find food,
clothing and medical attention, where necessary. But it is
doubtful whether such principles would be applied in their
full rigour today. The law is not static in this connection and
the courts are prepared to use the device of "terms implied
in law" to create something of a code for modern employment
when they are given the opportunity.

V ILLEGAL TERMS

In general, the law will not enforce illegal contracts: they
are void and may be disregarded. There are many varieties
of illegality. We are not here simply concerned with contracts
to commit a crime, but also with contracts with minor illegal
elements and even with immoral contracts or contracts which
the law, as a matter of policy, will not lend its aid to.

For practical purposes, there is no need to spend much time
on the obvious point that to employ a man to commit a crime
will not produce legal obligation. Nor will certain obvious types
of immoral contract of employment—those involving prostitu-
tion, for instance. The real problems arise in connection with
perfectly lawful contracts of employment that happen to have
illegal terms in them, and also in connection with principles
which declare certain matters to be "illegal" because they are
"against the policy of the law".

Provided that the illegal part of the contract is subsidiary and independent of the rest of the contract, they can be "severed" and the lawful part of the contract may stand without them. An employee whose duties involve any illegality may properly refuse to have any part of that illegality and remain employed.

There are two particular matters which are "against the policy of the law" which are relevant to the contract of employment. First there are "servile incidents". The law draws a line between service and servitude. If a contract of employment contains terms which restrict personal freedom, then those terms are illegal and of no effect. In modern times there are few examples of such terms and in each case the whole circumstances of the contract must be looked at. What would be an entirely unjustified infringement of liberty in one case may not be in another. In one case the court was prepared to uphold a term which imposed a limit upon the weight of an employee, because the employee was a highly paid film-star, whose weight and personal appearance were obviously commercially important to the employer (*Gaumont-British* v. *Alexander* (1936) KB). Such a clause would be quite unenforceable against a typist.

Secondly, the law has always regarded contracts "in restraint of trade" to be against public policy. In employment, this means contracts which restrict the freedom of the employee to work or do business wherever and in whatever trade he might wish. Of course, as was explained previously, according to general principle while an employee is in employment he may not act against the interests of his employers, by soliciting his customers, stealing his trade secrets or by acting in competition with him. So there is no need for an employer to try to protect his interests *during* employment. As a result, the clauses one has to deal with seek to impose restrictions upon the activities of employees *after* they leave their employment.

The main lines of the approach of the courts to this question were laid down in a case in 1896 (*Nordenfelt* v. *Maxim Nordenfelt and Co.* HL) in which a manufacturer of guns and ammunition sold his business to a company and, in return, promised never to engage in that trade anywhere in the world

for the rest of his life. It must have seemed most unlikely
that such an absolute restriction would be held enforceable,
but in the circumstances it was clearly a fair one. Otherwise
Mr. Nordenfelt would have been able to sell his business and
steal it back next year by trading in his own name. So the
House of Lords held the restraint valid and pronounced that
although restraints of trade were in principle illegal and unenforceable, they might be justified "if the restriction is reasonable—reasonable, that is, in reference to the interests of the
parties concerned and reasonable in reference to the interests
of the public" (*per* Lord MacNaghten).

In practice, one can disregard the second branch of this
test—it has always been difficult to argue the public interest
in the context of what is, essentially, a dispute between two
private individuals.

If the right of an employer to impose restrictions upon the
work which an ex-employee may do is to be tested by reference
to its "reasonableness in the interests of the parties", the
matter soon comes to the question of what interests of the
employer are to be recognised as reasonable. (The interests
of the employee are clear: his freedom to work as he wishes.)
And the courts have in fact recognised two types of interest.
The first is connected with customers, the second with trade
secrets.

Every business has its goodwill and it is a valuable asset.
Employees who have contact with customers can clearly
damage that goodwill if they wish, and so the employer is
given the right to protect that interest after the employment
has come to an end. There are two ways in which this is
commonly done. One is to restrict the activities of the ex-
employee in the trade in question in a given area. The risk
here is that an employer may try to get protection over a wider
area than is reasonable. So in one case an employer tried to
prevent a salesman from working in the trade within twenty-
five miles of London, which was an area in which the employer
traded. But the man in question had only come into contact
with customers in one district of London, so the court held
the restriction unreasonably wide (*Mason* v. *Provident Clothing and Supply Co.* (1913) HL). In short, an employer may

not restrict a man over more than his "patch", because to
do so would be to try and protect oneself against competition,
not to protect an identifiable interest.

Of recent years, however, it has become common to express
this sort of restriction in terms that the ex-employee should
not try to solicit any person who was a customer of the
employer during the period of employment. After some doubt,
it was established that this method was effective (*Plowman*
v. *Ash* (1964) CA).

Trade secrets are much easier to deal with. They include
inventions or new processes of the sort that could be patented
if the employer wishes. In practice, it is often more sensible to
protect the results of research in industry with good security
systems, supported by restrictions of this kind, than to use the
rather cumbrous methods of the Patents Act. In any event, it
is clear that it is no possible to protect the vague interests that
an employer might have in the organisation and methods of his
firm:

> A reporter was employed on terms that he would not
> afterwards make use of his employer's methods of organi-
> sation and sources of information. The restriction was
> unenforceable.
>
> *Leng* v. *Andrews* (1909) CA

Whether the subject-matter of the restriction be secrets
or customers, it must also be reasonable as to time. An
employer is not entitled to impose restrictions on an employee
for longer than is reasonably necessary—a vague yardstick
which will ultimately be based upon the length of time
it takes for customers to forget, or for a secret to become
well known, but in every case balanced against the need
not to restrict unduly the freedom of the individual.

Cases usually arise in this area when an employer seeks
an injunction (or more rarely damages) to prevent an ex-
employee from setting up in opposition or from taking employment with a competitor. His first task is to show that
the contract of employment still exists for this purpose. If
the employer has broken it, by wrongfully dismissing the

employee, then the contract has come to an end for all purposes (*General Billposting* v. *Atkinson* (1908) CA), but if it
has been properly terminated by notice or otherwise, then this
aspect of the contract remains in force.

If the restraint is unreasonable, then the employer will not
obtain a remedy. But it is sometimes possible to "sever" that
which is objectionable and enforce the cut-down remainder.
But before the court will allow this, it has to be shown that
the different parts of the clause can be separated without re-
drafting it. Employers, therefore, often have restraint clauses
drafted in the form of several different sub-clauses, each containing different restrictions, so that if one is found to be
unreasonable, the others may be enforced.

VI   STATUTORY CONTROL

The contract of employment is, in law, much affected by
a great variety of Acts of Parliament which have been passed
to establish minimum conditions of employment. Many of
these Acts of Parliament simply lay down their standards and
can be understood without regard to the existence of a contract
of employment (*e.g.* the Factories Act, the Offices, Shops and
Railway Premises Act, etc., which are dealt with under
"Employers' Liability" later in the book). Others, such as the
Contracts of Employment Act, the Redundancy Payments Act,
the Industrial Relations Act and the National Insurance Acts,
are dealt with in other parts of the book and, where necessary,
their relation to the contract of employment explained there.
There remain a number of Acts which deal with matters
which are still, in law, regulated primarily by the contract of
employment—these are hours of work and wages.

Hours of work are regulated by a series of very complicated
Acts of Parliament. There is no general rule: children (below
16) and young persons (16 to 18) are restricted both as to
where they may work (children, for example, may not be
employed in any factory, on a ship or underground in a mine)
and for how long (a young person may not work more
than a 48-hour week with very restricted overtime). Women

are subject to similar restrictions. Adult men only have their hours restricted in transport, shops, bakeries, sheet-glass manufacture and underground in coal mines. It is not possible to go into the details in a book of this nature.

Wages, too, are governed primarily by the contract. They are usually fixed by an express term, but a person employed to work with no express agreement as to wages will be entitled to the "going rate" by virtue of an implied term. Wages Councils, established under the Wages Councils Act 1959, and the Agricultural Wages Board, under the Agricultural Wages Act 1948, set minimum wages for nearly four million workers. Councils are established in trades where there is no adequate machinery for fixing wages, that is, the trades where union organisation is not strong. They may be wound up if the need for them seems to have ceased. They are representative bodies of employers and workers with independent chairmen. They make proposals for minimum wages, and for minimum annual paid holidays under the Holidays With Pay Act 1938, which they forward to the Minister. They may also report on other aspects of industrial relations in the trade for which they are established.

The Minister may accept a proposal from the Wages Council, or he may refer it back. But he may not amend it. If accepted, it is made as a Wages Regulation Order. The effect of this order is not only to make it a criminal offence for an employer in the trade to pay less, but also to amend every contract of employment so far as it provides for wages less than the minimum laid down by the order.

There is a great deal more law on how wages should be paid than there is on how much should be paid. The first Truck Act was passed in 1831 and the last in 1940. The main aim was to outlaw the system of "trucking" whereby workers were paid in goods or in tokens which could be exchanged for goods. Essentially, they provide that manual workers must be paid in cash without deductions other than those that are legally permitted. Most deductions that are allowed have little modern significance; but friendly society ("club") subscriptions may be deducted and "fines" for bad work, provided prior written consent is obtained. PAYE and National Insurance contributions are compulsorily deducted. No contract requiring a worker to spend his wages in a particular way is valid, and if an employer supplies goods to a worker on credit, he is not legally entitled to recover the price.

The Truck Acts apply only to manual workers: the practice grew, this century, of paying non-manual workers otherwise than in cash—by cheque, or direct bank payment, for example. The advantages of such a system from the security point of view are considerable and in 1960 the Payment of Wages Act sought to introduce the system as an option generally. Workers may be paid by cheque, postal order or by direct payment into a bank, provided that individual prior written consent (which the worker may unilaterally withdraw at any time) is obtained. The Act has not had a great effect.

There are other controls. Wages may not be paid in a public house (Payment of Wages in Public Houses Prohibition Act 1883); an employer may not have an interest in a "Shop Club" or "Christmas Club" run by his employees (Shop Clubs Act 1902). In industries, such as mining, where workers are traditionally paid by reference to material that must be weighed, "checkweighers" are appointed who are responsible to the workers, to supervise the weighing process. (Checkweighing in Various Industries Act 1919; see also the Factories Act 1961, s. 144(1), which provides for the keeping of accurate measuring equipment for the same reason.)

The Attachment of Earnings Act 1971 reverses a long-standing policy by opening wages to creditors of employees. Under its provisions, County Courts and Magistrates' Courts may make attachment orders directed to the employer to make deductions from wages to pay debts, fines, etc. Not only is the deduction rate specified, but a "protected earnings rate" below which wages are not to fall.

The Equal Pay Act 1970 is to come into force at the end of 1975. It implies into every woman's contract of employment a term that she shall be given "equal treatment with men in the same employment". This is clearly much wider than wages, but it is in connection with wages that it is most likely to be used. Disputes on an individual level are to go to the Industrial Tribunal, while any discriminatory collective agreements may be sent to the Industrial Arbitration Board.

Chapter 3

Termination of Employment

I THE COMMON LAW

There are four quite distinct legal questions that are immediately raised when employment is brought to an end. First,
was the contract properly terminated? Secondly, what are the
consequences if the contract has been terminated improperly?
Thirdly, was the employee dismissed for redundancy so as to
qualify for a redundancy payment under the Redundancy Payments Act 1965? Finally, was the termination fair or unfair
within the meaning of the Industrial Relations Act 1971?

To take the first question, contracts of employment are properly terminated by notice, dismissal for misconduct, the
expiry of a fixed-term contract or frustration.

(*a*) *Notice* is a surprisingly modern development in the law
of employment. The old rule was that a man employed indefinitely was taken to be employed for a year, at the end of which
he was notionally re-employed for a further year. Indeed, as
late as 1969 the Court of Appeal found it necessary to say that
this "yearly hiring" idea was no longer alive (*Richardson* v.
Koefod (1969) CA). But, for practical purposes, notice was
established by the beginning of this century. The principle
is that either party may lawfully terminate the contract by
giving the other "reasonable notice". Once done, the contract
will come to an end at the end of the notice period.

The right to give notice is implied into the contract as a
"term implied in law", and it is a very important term that
is very difficult to displace.

34

The plaintiff was appointed to a "permanent" post. She had a written contract of employment which contained a clause on termination. This clause gave her employers power to terminate her contract only for "gross misconduct" and unfitness for her work. She became redundant and was given notice. The House of Lords, by a bare majority, held that although most contracts of employment were terminable on notice, this one was a rare exception. This was not because the post was "permanent" but because in a long written contract a carefully drafted clause had dealt with termination exhaustively.

McClelland v. *N.I. General Health Services Board* (1957) HL

The length of notice that is sufficient for termination can be fixed by the contract. This may be by express term ("four weeks' notice on either side") or by the incorporation of a practice by means of an implied term.

If there is neither an express nor an implied term, then *reasonable* notice is what is required. What is reasonable depends largely upon the status of the worker. The courts did not, as a rule, require very long periods for ordinary weekly wage earners. Since 1963 the law has imposed minimum periods of notice, based upon years of continuous employment with the same employer (Contracts of Employment Act 1963, amended and now consolidated in the Contracts of Employment Act 1972). At present, these are:

An employee is entitled to receive:

> One week's notice after 13 weeks' continuous employment;
> Two weeks' notice after two years' continuous employment;
> Four weeks' notice after five years' continuous employment;
> Six weeks' notice after ten years' continuous employment;
> Eight weeks' notice after 15 years' continuous employment.

After 13 weeks' continuous employment, an employee must give at least one week's notice to his employer.

They are all minimum periods: they can be increased by the contract (or even by the Court, if what is "reasonable" is longer), but they cannot be reduced. Any contractual stipulation for less is automatically replaced. In practice, the statutory minimum periods are what very many employees are legally entitled to.

Notice, once given, cannot be withdrawn without the agreement of the other party (*Bryan* v. *George Wimpey* (1968) IT). The right to give notice is absolute and can be exercised at any time for any reason or for none at all. *Why* a man is dismissed, though a relevant question in some other contexts, is quite irrelevant here.

(*b*) *Misconduct* has always been a separate ground for terminating a contract of employment. This is true of both sides, and although in most cases it is likely to be the employer who dismisses the employee for misconduct it is as well to remember that equivalent misconduct by an employer entitles the employee to leave without notice. Although misconduct has a history that is closely connected with punishment for misbehaviour, it is simpler today to treat the legal issues as an application of certain general rules of the law of contract. For that is how the courts approach it.

If one party to a contract breaks it, the innocent party may have the right to call the whole contract off and release himself from further legal obligations under it. He will have this right only when the breach by the other party is so serious as to make proper performance impossible: when the breach "goes to the root of the contract". If A must pay £50 on the first of every month to B under a contract, five days' delay in one payment does not "go to the root" and will not be sufficient to entitle B to cancel the contract. On the other hand, failure to make any payments for, say, six months almost certainly will. Six months' delay means more than a temporary difficulty, it means that A is probably in the sort of financial state which will prevent him from ever keeping up the payments.

The same sort of principles can be applied to employment.

We must look for a breach of contract which is so serious
as to put the continuance of the relationship of employer and
employee in jeopardy. The moral quality of the behaviour is
not really important. It must be a breach of contract, either
of the express terms or of the implied terms described in the
last chapter. And it must be such as to indicate that the party
in breach will not continue to perform satisfactorily. For this,
a good rule of thumb is to ask how often the behaviour
occurred. Being late once, swearing at a supervisor once, indicates very little, but regular bad timekeeping and regular insub-
ordination mean an unsatisfactory employee. But "you can
do it once, but not twice" is only a rule of thumb. A single
act of carelessness (say of a railway signalman) could have
results so catastrophic, and therefore be so important, as to
constitute good grounds for instant dismissal:

> A secretary accompanied her boss to a meeting with the
> managing director. There was an argument. Her boss
> left the room, and she followed. The managing director
> ordered her to stay and, when she refused, dismissed her
> instantly. The court held that her action did not justify
> instant dismissal: she was not repudiating her contractual
> responsibilities, she was merely caught in a conflict of
> loyalties and had made the wrong decision.

Laws v. *London Chronicle* (1959) CA

> A betting-shop manager took £10 from the till, honestly
> intending to replace it later. He had been warned not
> to do this. This was held sufficient grounds for instant
> dismissal, since his act was done in the sight of junior
> staff and was subversive of discipline, as well as having
> been done in open defiance of a specific order.

Sinclair v. *Neighbour* (1967) CA

In addition, it is always possible to insert additional terms
into the contract which specify situations in which the penalty
of instant dismissal may be exacted. Then, so long as this
term has properly become part of the contract, the employer
may dismiss without notice if the situation arises.

In law, the only disciplinary right which misconduct gives
to the employer is the right to dismiss without notice. For
in law all he is doing is bringing the contract to an end because
of the other's serious breach. There is no power to suspend
(*Hanley* v. *Pease and Partners* (1915) DC) nor to fine unless
there is an agreed term in the contract to that effect. A fine,
even permitted by the contract, being a deduction from wages,
may be subject to the provisions of the Truck Acts.

(*c*) If a man is employed for a fixed period—say a year—his
contract automatically comes to an end at the expiry of that
period and if he continues to be employed it can only be by
a further contract. As was mentioned earlier, this used to be
the general analysis of the situation when a man was employed
indefinitely, but this is no longer the case. Fixed-term contracts are not very common, but they do occur. One example
is probationary employment. The legal position is quite clear:
no notice is required to terminate the agreement at the due
date, indeed the contract will terminate "of its own accord"
unless the parties do something about it. During the period
the contract may be terminated in the usual way by notice
or, in a proper case, instantly.

(*d*) *Frustration* is the doctrine of the law of contract which
lays down that if events which are outside the control of the
parties occur which render the further performance of a contract impossible then it automatically comes to an end at that
point. The important word is "impossible". The fact that a
contract is more difficult to perform, or more expensive, is
of no account.

In employment the only examples of frustration that have
any importance are death and disablement. Death of an
employee clearly puts a contract of employment to an end:
it is a contract of personal service and cannot be performed
by anyone else. Death of an employer in these days of companies generally means winding-up:

> A miner was employed by Hickleton Main Colliery Co.
> Ltd. Under a reorganisation scheme that company was
> wound up and all its "property and rights" were trans-
> ferred to a company called Doncaster Colleries Ltd. It

was held that he was not employed by Doncaster Collieries Ltd. His contract with Hickleton Main had automatically come to an end (by frustration) when that company had been wound up. He had never agreed to work for Doncaster Collieries.

Nokes v. *Doncaster Colleries Ltd.* (1940) HL

By disablement is meant more than physical disablement: any condition which makes it impossible for the employment to continue, such as the internment of an employee by an enemy government (*Horlock* v. *Beal* (1916) HL). On the employer's side an equivalent might be the stopping of the business for which the worker was employed, provided that this was not brought about by an act of the employer (and closing down a business, or selling it, because it had become unprofitable would not amount to frustration). As was mentioned in the last chapter, sickness of an employee could bring a contract of employment to an end if it was such as to prevent further performance. Usually, this will not be so. In one case an illness lasting for six years was held not to be sufficient to frustrate the contract (*Cuckson* v. *Stones* (1858) QB):

> A pop-group drummer collapsed and was medically advised that if he continued with the group (who played seven nights a week) he would run a serious risk of schizophrenia. He might, however, play three or four nights a week. His contract lasted for five years. It was held frustrated.

Condor v. *The Barron Knights Ltd.* (1966) QB

II   WRONGFUL DISMISSAL

Before the Industrial Relations Act the only remedy available for a dismissed employee was an action for breach of contract, usually called an action for wrongful dismissal. Generally these actions are actions for damages.

As we have said, the common law allows an employer to dismiss an employee at any time, for any reason or none, provided only that he gives proper notice. So the only way an employee may be dismissed in breach of contract will be if he is given no notice, or less notice than he is entitled to (subject, of course, to any effective provision which guarantees him security of employment). Damages for breach of contract are, in general, such money compensation as will make up the difference between the contract as broken and the contract as performed. If A is entitled to three weeks' notice and is dismissed instantly, this difference is three weeks' wages, since he could have been dismissed quite properly at that cost. Further, an innocent party to a broken contract is legally obliged to "mitigate his loss", that is, to take whatever course of action reduces the loss. If he does not, then he must bear the consequences. A successful plaintiff in an action for wrongful dismissal will therefore be awarded damages based upon wages for the notice period less whatever he earned, or ought reasonably to have earned, in available work during that period. The amount is not likely to be high.

Often employees who are to be dismissed are offered "wages in lieu of notice"—that is, wages for the notice period. If this offer is accepted, then the contract has been brought to an end by agreement. Strictly speaking, an employee could refuse such an offer and insist upon working out his notice, but if his employer resisted, the employee's right to damages would rarely exceed what he had rejected and so it would seldom be worth while.

As was explained in the previous chapter, contracts of employment cannot be directly enforced by court order. One aspect of this rule is reinforced by the Industrial Relations Act 1971, s. 128, which enacts that "no court shall . . . compel an employee to do any work or to attend at any place for the purpose of doing any work". The converse rule is equally strict, though it is not found in the Industrial Relations Act. Courts may not compel an employer to employ.

This general rule is subject to two exceptions, or apparent exceptions. It does not apply to those whose employment is coupled with an office. They may be granted court orders restraining their employers from depriving them of that office in a legally improper way. The principle has been applied to chief constables (*Ridge* v. *Baldwin* (1964) HL) and registered dock workers (*Vine* v. *National Dock Labour Board* (1957) HL) but not to university professors (*Vidyodaya University of Ceylon* v. *Silva* (1964) PC). It is clearly a difficult distinction to make.

> A full-time official of a trade union was, in breach of his contract, dismissed from his post and expelled from his union. The court issued orders which, in effect, reinstated him in the union, but, as regards his employment, he was awarded damages only.
>
> *Taylor* v. *National Union of Seamen* (1967) QB

Secondly, in exceptional cases it may be possible to obtain an injunction restraining an employer from acting on an unlawful notice of termination. This was done in a recent case, *Hill* v. *C. A. Parsons Ltd.* (1971) CA, in which an employee was given one month's notice. The court felt that this was far too short for a man in his position, six months being closer to the mark. He was able to begin proceedings before the notice had expired, which was essential, since the court made it clear that it would not interfere if the employee had ceased being employed, however wrongfully that had been brought about. Moreover, the employer in this case was under union pressure and was not himself insistent upon the departure of the plaintiff. Such cases will be rare, but they are still possible.

III   REDUNDANCY

Until 1965 reasons for dismissal were legally irrelevant in England. An employer might dismiss a man for any reason or for none at all: all the law asked was that he gave adequate notice. In 1965 a slight dent was made in that principle by the Redundancy Payments Act. The aim of this legislation was to compensate those made redundant by a cash payment calculated by reference to the length of time the person declared redundant had been "continuously employed" by his employer. The benefits are paid by the employer, who may claim a rebate from a fund supported by payments made by employer and employee through the National Insurance stamp. Any person who feels entitled to a payment may appeal to the local Industrial Tribunal.

When a claim is made for a redundancy payment, any of three questions may have to be decided: was the applicant dismissed within the meaning of the Act; was he dismissed for redundancy; and to how much is he entitled?

(1) Dismissal

The Act is concerned with the *reasons* for dismissal, not primarily with the *method*. But a man is only entitled if he has been *dismissed*, not if he has left voluntarily. So the Act covers termination by the employer with notice and without notice (whether such action was justified by the employee's misconduct or not) and the non-renewal of a fixed-term contract (s. 3(1)). It goes further: even if the employee did leave voluntarily, he is not deprived of his rights if he was "forced out"—that is, if his termination of the contract was legally justified by his employer's conduct (s. 3(1)(*c*)). This brings in many considerations. As was pointed out earlier, the basic principle is that an employee is entitled to leave without notice in the same sort of circumstances as an employer is entitled to dismiss without notice: where the other (in this case the employer) has committed a serious breach of contract which puts the future of the contract in jeopardy. Failure to pay the agreed wages is a good example, as is failure to provide an opportunity to earn bonuses, etc. (*Ramage* v. *Harper-Mackay Ltd.* (1966) IT). Moreover, if an employer exceeds his contractual rights by, for example, requiring employees to work at a place they were not obliged to, or at different work from that for which they were employed, this too amounts to a legal justification for leaving. Of course, in such cases, it has to be shown that what was asked of the employee was in truth more than what he was legally obliged to do. This can be a complicated question.

A man was taken on as a day-worker but after fifteen months transferred to the night shift where he worked for twelve years. He left when his employers proposed to put him on the day shift. The Tribunal held that his employer had not exceeded his rights and the applicant's leaving was not to be counted as a dismissal.

Jones v. *Youngman Ltd.* (1966) IT

In addition to these cases of dismissal, the Act counts certain other situations as dismissals. These are "any act on the part of the employer" and "any event affecting the employer" which terminate the employment (s. 22(1)). These are very general words, but in practice they cover cases where the employer dies or, if a company, is put into certain types of receivership or liquidation. The law on this point is rather complicated: broadly, compulsory winding-up orders and court-appointed receiverships terminate employment contracts, as does the death of a personal employer. In the last case only does the Act provide that an employee whose contract is renewed within eight weeks of his employer's death (by the employer's personal representative) is not "dismissed": but there is no such provision for the other cases where employees may perhaps continue in fact in their jobs but be "dismissed" for the purposes of the Act. Voluntary winding-up and receivers acting on behalf of the company do not affect the contracts of employment of the employees (though such employees are, of course, very likely to find themselves dismissed in a more normal sort of way).

Warning is not dismissal: so where an employer warned an employee of likely redundancy, and he left to find other work, he had not been "dismissed" for redundancy (*Morton Sundour Fabrics* v. *Shaw* (1967) DC). On the other hand, if an employee is told that he will be dismissed at a future date, no matter how far in the future, this *is* dismissal (see *Hicks* v. *Humphrey* (1967) IT). If a man under notice for redundancy wishes to leave before its expiry (to get other work) his status as a dismissed person will not be lost if he gives written notice of his intention and this is accepted by his employer (Redundancy Payments Act, s. 4).

(2) **Redundancy**

This is defined fairly simply in s. 1 of the Act. There are three types of redundancy: (a) that brought about when an employer ceases to carry on the business for which the applicant was employed; (b) that brought about by the employer ceasing to carry on business in the place where the applicant was employed; and (c) that brought about by the reduction in the requirement of the business for employees to carry out a particular type of work.

Although it is for the applicant to prove that he was dismissed, the Act shifts the burden of disproving the redundancy to the employer (s. 9(2) (b)). This means two things: first, that if the evidence is doubtful and the tribunal cannot make up its mind, the benefit of the doubt goes to the applicant; secondly, that if the employer offers no explanation at all for dismissing the applicant, the presumption is made in the applicant's favour and he gets his payment.

Redundancy caused by ceasing to do business is not difficult to identify, but redundancy caused by ceasing to do business at a particular place raises more difficult problems. It all turns on where the applicant was employed to work. Some people are specifically taken on to work at one defined place; others, particularly in the construction industry, are clearly employed as "travelling men" to work at a variety of places as the work is available. But very many cases fall between the two extremes and pose a difficult question of fact for the tribunal.

Redundancy caused by a reduction in labour requirements may take one of two main forms. It may simply be that trade is declining; or the business might be reorganised so as to reduce labour costs or to change the emphasis of the work. In either case, a good rule-of-thumb to start with is to ask the question whether the dismissed employee was or was not replaced. If he was replaced, this does not look like redundancy: if he was not, it does. But the cases can get very complicated:

> Mr. Skimins was a sales representative. His employers decided to reduce operations in his territory, but instead

of dismissing him transferred him to the office and later promoted him to warehouse manager. This displaced Mr. Spurrett, who was held redundant.

W. Gimber and Sons v. *Spurrett* (1967) DC

Mr. Mackenzie was a cost accountant with few paper qualifications. A new system of budgetary control was introduced which his employers felt he would not be able to cope with. He was replaced by a qualified man. He was not redundant, merely wanting in skill.

Mackenzie v. *William Paton Ltd.* (1966) IT

Mrs. Loudon was a crisp packer: she was not young. Faster crisp packing machines were introduced and the older packers were dismissed as being too slow to operate them. She was redundant: the need for slow packing machine operators had diminished.

Loudon v. *Crimpy Crisps* (1966) IT

Clearly the lines are difficult, if not impossible, to draw.

A redundant employee will not be entitled to a redundancy payment if his employer offered to renew his employment on the same terms, before the dismissal was effective, or made him an offer, *in writing*, of "suitable alternative employment". In either case, if the redundant worker refuses the offer, he is not entitled to a payment and, almost as important, he loses the benefit of the accrued years of service with that employer in calculating any payment in the future. If he accepts such an offer (and there may be difficulties in deciding whether he has, in truth, done so), then he is treated as not having been dismissed. Clearly, "suitable alternative employment" provides a fertile field for argument.

Finally, there are complicated provisions designed to prevent employers avoiding their responsibilities under the Act by using lay-off and short-time in preference to dismissal for redundancy. In essence, these allow an employee put on short-time or laid off for a substantial period to serve notice that he is claiming a redundancy payment and then to leave and retain his entitlement notwithstanding the fact that he has not been "dismissed". There are many formal requirements (Redundancy Payments Act, ss. 6, 7).

(3) Payment

A redundancy payment is not compensation: it is a small "golden handshake" payable only in the narrow circumstances of redundancy. It is calculated by multiplying the years of continuous service the redundant employee has put in with that employer by one and a half, one, or half a week's pay when he is dismissed. The choice of the multiplier depends upon age. Wages over £40 per week are disregarded. This gives a theoretical maximum of £1,200, but the average payments are much less. The employer is entitled to a rebate of one-half from the fund.

What is important is *continuous* employment with the same employer. Once a man changes his job, or is dismissed, or even in some cases where he keeps his job, but the business for which he works is taken over by someone else, then the continuity of his employment is broken. As there is no entitlement at all for the first two years of employment and even afterwards entitlement builds up very slowly, the matter is serious.

Of course, if continuity was broken by dismissal for redundancy, and a claim was made, nothing is lost. But there are many other reasons for losing a job, and even when there is redundancy, claims must be made within six months.

Continuity of employment means continuity of a *contract* of employment: so long as the contract continues, entitlement mounts up. So absence from work through holidays, sickness, short-term lay-off, or even perhaps disciplinary suspension, does not affect continuity:

Mr. Marshall had been employed by Harland and Wolff for 23 years when he was struck down by angina pectoris. He never returned to work and, in accordance with his contract, received no sick-pay. Twenty-one months later, the employer closed down the yard where Mr. Marshall had worked. He was held redundant and entitled to his full payment, calculated by reference to all his years of employment: the sickness, though severe, had not frustrated his contract, which continued.

Marshall v. *Harland and Wolff* (1972) NIRC

It may be that some interruptions of work do affect the contract of employment. In the case of lay-off, for example, the practice of the trade might be that the laid-off men are dismissed and re-employed after the reason for lay-off has passed: equally, they could be kept on the books. To make the matter a little more rational, the Act steps in in six cases and declares that, whether the contract is terminated or not, continuity shall not be broken. The circumstances are:

> sickness or injury;
> temporary cessation of work: there is no specific length
> of time here. All that matters is that there should be
> no work for the employee to do (*Fitzgerald* v. *Hall
> Russell* (1970) HL) and that the situation turned out not
> to be permanent (*Hunter* v. *Smith's Dock* (1968) DC;
> absence by special arrangement or custom;
> national service;
> employment outside the U.K.;
> strikes and lock-outs.

In respect of the last three events, the period spent away from work is not counted towards the total of years served. To this, again, there is an exception: time spent on strike or locked out before 6th July, 1964 (when the Act came into operation), is counted towards the total. In the first three cases, the time spent away from work does count towards the total.

IV UNFAIR DISMISSAL

If the Redundancy Payments Act made a dent in the principle that a man might be dismissed for no reason without legal consequences, the Industrial Relations Act 1971 is a frontal assault. In this Act the Government has sought to give

effect to ILO Recommendation 119, of 1964, long accepted
by successive British Governments.

The basic principle is to be found in s. 22: "every employee
shall have the right not to be unfairly dismissed by his
employer". A person who feels that he has been unfairly dismissed may appeal to an industrial tribunal: the tribunal, if
satisfied that the case is proved, may award compensation and,
in appropriate cases, recommend reinstatement. The period
during which appeals may be made is short—only four weeks—
but in practice nearly every employee has been given the right
to have the reasons for his dismissal examined and tested
against standards of "fairness". The most important group
excluded are those with less than two years' employment
(except when dismissed on account of trade union activities),
but other less important groups, such as those closely related
to the employer and those employed in very small undertak-
ings, are also excluded. Crown servants, surprisingly, are
included.

"Dismissal" is not defined in so complicated a way as in
the Redundancy Payments Act: termination by the employer,
with or without notice, the non-renewal of a fixed-term contract and an employee under notice giving counter-notice to
his employer are the only situations covered. The problems that
have arisen have largely been time problems. There are two
practical questions: the first is whether the employee had two
years' service before the "effective date of termination", for
without it he does not qualify for protection; the second is
whether he made his claim within the very short limitation
period of four weeks (which the Tribunal has virtually no discretion to extend) from the "effective date of termination".
Most cases are easy: the man turned off the premises without
notice is "effectively terminated" on that day; the man whose
contract expired on 1st June and was not renewed was "effectively terminated" on 1st June. But others are harder. A man
who accepts wages in lieu of notice is dismissed when he
accepts the money, not when the notice expires (*Dixon* v.
Stenor (1973) NIRC): but an employee given notice and told
to "take a holiday" is dismissed when the notice expires
(*Brindle* v. *H. W. Smith* (1973) CA).

A dismissed employee may appeal to the Industrial Tribunal (Industrial Relations Act, s. 106). It is for the employer to show what the reason for the dismissal was. If he fails to do this, then the dismissal is taken to be unfair. The employer must then show that the reason was a fair one. The Act lays down four "good" reasons and the employer might try to show that the dismissal came within one of these. In addition, the Act permits the employer to show that he had "some other substantial reason of a kind such as to justify the dismissal of an employee holding a position which that employee held".

The four "good" reasons are:

(i) *Reasons "related to the capability or qualifications of the employee for performing work of the kind which he was employed by the employer to do"*. The Act makes clear (in s. 25(7)) that "capability" includes "skill, aptitude, health or any other physical or mental quality", which covers illness, age and even lack of good looks, as well as lack of technical ability or intelligence. Of course, these factors must be directly related to the job. "Qualifications", on the other hand, are more narrowly explained: the term seems to be confined to degrees, diplomas and other paper qualifications. The Code of Practice (which must be taken into account where relevant) has little to say at this point. There are, however, three paragraphs on training (33–35) and two (26, 27) which require the promotion by management of equal opportunity in employment, which might well be relevant in some cases.

(ii) *Reasons "related to the conduct of the employee"*. At common law it was always justifiable for an employer to dismiss an employee without notice for a serious breach of contract. This was generally called "misconduct" and there can be little doubt that the idea behind this provision of the Industrial Relations Act is much the same. The Code of Practice has a whole section (paras. 130–133) devoted to disciplinary procedures. These require that an employer should agree a written procedure with trade unions and should make it known to all employees (paras. 130, 131). The procedure should set out who has authority to impose which disciplinary sanction and place the power of dismissal at a level higher than the employee's immediate supervisor; should give the employee a hearing, with a representative if he wishes; and should provide for an appeal and possibly for final referral to arbitration (para. 132). Finally, the Code sets out several points for guidance in the use of disciplinary procedures (para. 133). The first step should be an oral warning, or a written warning for more serious matters—except in very serious cases, no one should be dismissed for the first "offence". Action, such as disciplinary suspension or dismissal, should be recorded in writing, and details given to the employee and, if necessary, his shop steward. Shop stewards should only be disciplined after discussions with full-time officials. Employers complying with this recommended system would generally have a fairly formal system of dealing with disciplinary problems, with comprehensive written records and several stages to be gone through for each type of "offence". The extent to which an employer does or does not use such a system is clearly relevant to "reasons related to the conduct of the employee" not only as to the *method* of dismissal (which will be discussed shortly), but also indirectly with the substance of what amounts to "conduct" which justifies dismissal.

(iii) *That the employee was redundant.* If a man is dismissed for redundancy, he is entitled to a redundancy payment. In many cases, then, it would seem reasonable that he should not receive compensation for unfair dismissal. Both matters are dealt with in the industrial tribunal, although the limitation periods are not the same (four weeks for unfair dismissal, six months for redundancy) and the amounts receivable are very different. However, as will be described shortly, the existence of a "good" reason does not necessarily settle the question of the fairness of the dismissal. So a man may receive both redundancy payment and compensation for unfair dismissal.

(iv) *That it would be illegal to employ the employee at the work in question.* It is illegal to employ children underground in mining: this provides a "good" reason for dismissing a child so employed.

If an employer fails to convince the tribunal that his reasons for dismissing the employee were within these four headings, or that they constituted "other substantial reasons", then the tribunal will hold the employee to have been unfairly dismissed. But if the employer is successful, that is not the end of the story. The tribunal proceeds to decide whether the dismissal was unfair "having regard to the reason shown by the employer" on the basis of whether "in all the circumstances he acted reasonably or unreasonably in treating it as a sufficient reason" for dismissal. This it must decide "in accordance with equity and the substantial merits of the case" (s. 25(6)). All of which gives the tribunal a very wide descretion. A man be incapable of keeping up with new techniques, but was it reasonable to dismiss him for that? Could he not have been found other work? Was it not the employer's fault anyway, for not giving proper opportunities for re-training? Everything is open for argument. But three points might be made.

(*a*) Particularly in relation to dismissal for reasons connected with conduct (but not only there), there may be a problem of relating method to reason. Given the existence, in the Code of Practice, of a fairly detailed scheme for a written disciplinary procedure, a dismissal by an employer who does not have such a procedure, or who does not act in accordance with the general guidelines as laid down, stands a fair chance of being held to be unfair even when the reasons are good. Equally, a man dismissed for redundancy with no advance warning and in humiliating circumstances seems to have a good claim. There is thus something of a distinction in practice between a dismissal for a bad reason and a dismissal for a good reason that was unfair because of the way it was done.

(*b*) When a man is dismissed for redundancy the question of whether it was fair is narrower than in other cases. Someone had to go, the only question being whether it should have been this man. The Act gives some help here (s. 25(5)) by laying down that it shall be regarded as unfair if he was chosen for redundancy either because he had exercised, or wished to exercise, any of his "entrenched" rights of trade union membership and activity (which are described in Chapter 6) or if he was chosen in breach of a "customary arrangement or agreed procedure". But this is not exhaustive: the tribunal must in every case of redundancy consider whether it was fair to choose the employee in question, even if there was no breach of procedure of interference with trade union rights (*Green* v. *Southampton Corporation* (1973) NIRC). So failure to give advance warning could make dismissal for redundancy unfair (see *Clarkson International Tools* v. *Short* (1973) NIRC).

But the relationship between the two questions of redundancy and unfairness can be very complicated:

> Miss Moppett was a working manageress at a special shoe shop. She was dismissed by a purchaser of the business who re-organised the business so as not to employ a working manageress but alleged that Miss Moppett had been inefficient. In the tribunal, the employer was not able to convince the court that this reason was true. NIRC held (i) that under the Redundancy Payments Act, in absence of proof of reason, Miss Moppett must be presumed to be dismissed for redundancy and so entitled to a payment; (ii) the presumption of redundancy only applied for the purposes of redundancy payments: for the purposes of unfair dismissal, in the absence of a proved reason, Miss Moppett was unfairly dismissed and entitled to compensation.

Midland Foot Comfort Centre v. *Moppett* (1973) NIRC

(*c*) The Act provides specifically that if an employee was dismissed for the reason, or principal reason, that he exercised, or wished to exercise, his entrenched trade union rights, then his dismissal is always unfair (s. 25(4)). These rights are not wide and their ambit has been narrowed by the fact that in many cases the union in question is not registered under the Industrial Relations Act. However, to dismiss a man because of the legitimate exercise of his functions as a shop steward of his union, even when that union is not registered, is clearly against the general policy of the Act (see s. 1(1)) and of the Code of Practice (see in particular the introduction, but the need to recognise the existence of unions and to deal with them pervades the whole Code). So dismissal because of union activities may be unfair on general grounds even when the union is unregistered (see *Kenyon* v. *Fred Millar* (1972) NIRC).

The Act deals specially with dismissals in connection with industrial action. There are two situations. First, the employer might dismiss employees in furtherance of his own ends in an industrial dispute. This is a lock-out within the meaning of the Act. Such a dismissal is not unfair, but if the employer does not re-engage the employees, then it may be. Similarly, if some employees are re-engaged but not others, those discriminated against can have the reasons for that discrimination examined in the industrial tribunal in the same way as if it were a case of dismissal. Secondly, an employer might dismiss all or some employees because they took part in a strike or other "irregular industrial action" within the meaning of the Act. (These terms are explained in Chapter 8.) If an employer dismisses all the strikers and either re-engages all of them afterwards, or re-engages none of them, then his actions are *not* to be treated as unfair dismissals. But if he discriminates, either by only dismissing some, or by only re-engaging some, then his discrimination may be treated as an unfair dismissal, but *only* if the reasons were that the employees discriminated against had exercised or threatened to exercise their "entrenched rights". Any other reason will, apparently, serve to render the employer's action fair within the meaning of the Act.

Once a complaint of unfair dismissal is lodged with a tribunal, conciliation officers of the Department of Employment are available to try to produce an agreed settlement. Should they fail, and should the complaint be found proved, the tribunal must give a remedy. It has three available. The first is of no practical importance: it may declare the legal rights of the parties. The second is an award of compensation, in practice the usual remedy.

Unlike redundancy payments, there is no scale. Instead s. 116 of the Act apparently gives an enormously wide discretion:

"... the amount ... shall ... be such ... as the ... tribunal considers just and equitable in all the circum-

stances, having regard to the loss sustained by the
aggrieved party . . ."

The section goes on to state that where the aggrieved party
contributed to his own damage, it shall be open to the tribunal
to reduce the compensation "to such extent . . . as the tribunal
considers just and equitable". Finally, there is a maximum
limit of £4,160 or two years' pay, whichever is the less (s.
118(1)).

The general effect of these provisions might be thought to
be to enable tribunals to put common-sense principles of fair-
play and justice into effect and to set compensation at levels
which reflect what they think of the behaviour of both sides to
the dispute. Certainly, the provisions take the tribunals a long
way away from the restricted "wages for the notice period"
approach of the common law. And to an extent this is true.
Tribunals and NIRC do reduce awards to those whose behaviour brought about their own dismissal (see, for instance,
s. 116(4) and *Winterhalter Gastronom Ltd.* v. *Webb* (1973)
NIRC), sometimes going to very great lengths:

> Mr. Earl's work had given his employers cause for con-
> cern. Then he was away ill. On the day of his return,
> he was handed a letter which, without previous warning,
> informed him of his dismissal. NIRC held that there was
> a good reason for his dismissal, although the method was
> grossly unfair. They held the dismissal unfair but
> awarded no compensation.

> *Earl* v. *Slater Wheeler (Airline) Ltd.* (1973) NIRC

However, in one case, *Norton Tool* v. *Tewson* (1973) NIRC,
the court took the opportunity to lay down general principles
upon which this wide discretion should be exercised. And
these principles are relatively narrow and closely related to the
"cash loss" approach of the common law. The argument that
NIRC accepted was that "compensation" must always be compensation for hard economic loss and that the wide discretion
must always be exercised "having regard to" that economic
loss, and not having regard to anything else.

Mr. Tewson, aged 50, was "abruptly" dismissed after 11 years' service. The tribunal found his dismissal unfair and the bulk of its award of compensation was expressed to be related to the "abruptness" and to the fact of his 11 years' service. The employers appealed. NIRC awarded compensation under four heads:

1	Immediate loss of wages—for the proper notice period:	£153–60
2	The manner of his dismissal *insofar as it could give rise to any risk of financial loss*:	£ NIL
3	Future loss of earnings—*e.g.* if his new job paid less or was less secure:	£ NIL
4	Loss of statutory protection:	
	(*a*) The Redundancy Payments Act. Mr. Tewson had 11 years' entitlement—£380 if he had been declared redundant then—and would have to start afresh:	£200
	(*b*) Unfair dismissal. For the first two years in his new job he would have no claim for unfair dismissal:	£ 20

NIRC rounded the figure up to £375.   £373–60

The Tewson analysis has become the basis upon which tribunals now award compensation in unfair dismissal cases. The approach throughout is "cash-loss related" and in general the effect seems to have been to fix the level of compensation.

Finally, the tribunal has the power to *recommend* that an unfairly dismissed employee should be reinstated (s. 116(4)). Logically, this comes before compensation, but it has much less practical importance. If a recommendation is made but is not complied with the tribunal then proceeds to fix the compensation. At this stage it is specifically directed to increase the amount if the employer has unreasonably refused to comply with the recommendation, and conversely to reduce them if it is the employee who has been unreasonable (s. 116(4)).

Chapter 4

The National Insurance System

THE PRINCIPLES OF THE SCHEME

National Insurance is based upon the simple premise that certain risks attendant upon employment ought to be covered by insurance and that it is not sensible to leave this to individual action. The scheme has its origins in the Workmen's Compensation Acts. The first of these was passed in 1897 and was designed to remedy the defects then existing in the law of employers' liability. To provide an employee injured at work with the guarantee of at least some compensation, employers were made responsible for "personal injuries caused by accidents arising out of and in the course of the employment" of their workers irrespective of fault. Employers were required to insure against the risk of having to make the small payments the Act required them to make by way of compensation for these injuries. The original scheme had defects, the benefits were small, the law was confused and the litigation fierce, but the principle had been established that the State might require risks of employment to be insured against.

In 1946 the scheme was re-worked as part of the overall plan of social insurance recommended by the Beveridge Report. The task was taken from private insurers and undertaken by the State. Premiums, in the form of stamps purchased from the Post Office and stuck onto official cards, are paid by "contributors" to the scheme. Even by 1946, the narrow ambit of the Workmen's Compensation Acts had been extended and the scheme now covers far more than industrial injury: sickness and unemployment being two other important risks that are covered. The system is as much a matter of state welfare as insurance. It is not funded like an insurance policy and benefits are paid directly from current income. This is supplemented by funds raised from general taxation, so the "premiums" have to be increased regularly to keep pace with increase in benefits. But tradition decreees that it be called insurance and formally treated as such.

Tradition also requires that the industrial injury aspects of national insurance be separately dealt with. There are two Acts, at present the National Insurance Act 1965 and the National Insurance (Industrial Injuries) Act 1965. In line with this, industrial injuries will be dealt with separately in this chapter.

Since 1946, there has only been one change of any importance. That is the introduction of the graduated principle, whereby certain contributions and benefits have been increased for higher-paid employees by sums calculated by reference to the level of their earnings. Rates of contribution and benefit are constantly changed, however, and we shall not attempt to give figures which will almost inevitably be out-of-date. Readers are referred to the most recent edition of the appropriate Ministry leaflet.

II CONTRIBUTORS AND CONTRIBUTIONS

For all national insurance purposes except industrial injuries, the population is divided into three classes of contributors:

Class I: persons gainfully employed under a contract of service;

Class II: other persons gainfully employed (self-employed);

Class III: all others above school-leaving and below retiring age (non-employed).

There are, however, exemptions. For example, the unemployed in receipt of unemployment benefit and the sick in receipt of sickness benefit are exempt from contributions, as are those married women (the majority) who have elected to "go on their husband's stamp".

There are two sorts of contributions. Flat-rate contributions are paid by all contributors: graduated contributions, expressed as a percentage of earnings above one level and below another, are payable only by Class I contributors who have not contracted out of that part of the scheme. In respect of Class I contributors, the contribution is expressed in part as the employer's contribution and in part as the employee's contribution. But employers are primarily responsible for the collection of both parts and are permitted to make the appropriate deductions from wages (despite the provisions of the Truck Acts).

As mentioned before, payments are made by affixing stamps to official cards, which belong to the Ministry and which must be exchanged, properly stamped up for each week, for a new one every year. The stamp is a useful method of collection for taxes and levies on employment: it contains contributions to the Redundancy Payments Fund, the Industrial Training Levy and, until its abolition, Selective Employment Tax.

III   BENEFITS

Apart from industrial injury benefits, the national insurance system provides for a multiplicity of benefits, supplements, allowances and pensions. They fall into four main groups: unemployment benefit, sickness benefit, widows' pensions and old age pensions. The last two are so much part of general state welfare that they can justifiably be omitted from a book on employment. The first two are more obviously linked.

Basically, sickness benefit is payable for 168 days to those qualified by having paid six months' contributions, who are incapacitated for work through sickness. To both periods mentioned there are qualifications, complications and exceptions. No benefit is paid for the first three days. After the 168 days, the claimant must requalify by making 13 weeks' contributions. A person must show that he is incapable of work—which is usually a matter of expert medical opinion. It is possible to be disqualified from sickness benefit for periods of up to six weeks. Disqualification may be on grounds of misconduct (*e.g.* voluntary misuse of drugs) or failure, without good cause, to submit to medical examination or take advantage of medical treatment.

Unemployment benefit does not depend upon incapacity, but upon the mere fact of not being in "gainful occupation". Any employment, or self-employment, will disqualify, unless its amount or returns are so negligible as to be disregarded. An unemployed person is, however, only entitled to unemployment benefit if his previous employment has been terminated. By a strange quirk of legalism, a person in receipt of payment in lieu of notice, and similar sums in compensation for lost employment, is considered still to be employed until the date on which the "notice" expires.

There are disqualifications from unemployment benefit, too. An employee dismissed for misconduct may be disqualified for a period of up to six weeks, as may a person who has left his employment voluntarily, except when he had "just cause" to leave. This last qualification causes great difficulties in its application: the applicant must show the circumstances which, in his view, gave grounds for his leaving and hope to convince the authorities that they were reasonable. The cases show no firm principles. Every case is dealt with on its own special facts. Applicants may also be disqualified, in the same way, for refusing, without good cause, to apply for a vacancy officially notified to him, or to take it if offered, or generally for neglecting to take reasonable steps to obtain suitable employment. All these clearly turn upon what, in all the circumstances, can be counted as suitable employment, so as to make refusal of it unreasonable. Again, the matter is always a question of fact, and a complicated one.

Finally, as a general policy, those who are not working on account of industrial action are not entitled to unemployment benefit. This is not a question of an essentially discretionary, temporary disqualification. It is permanent and automatic. The principle is that the State should not be called upon to finance, even indirectly, industrial action. At the same time, the employment exchange system with which unemployment benefit is intimately connected, preserves a careful neutrality. A man cannot be penalised for refusing work made available by a stoppage (*i.e.* for refusing to be a blackleg), nor do the exchanges refuse facilities for strikers who express a wish to find work while on strike.

Section 22 of the National Insurance Act 1965 (as amended by the Industrial Relations Act) lays down sweepingly that a man is permanently disqualified from receiving unemployment benefit if he lost his employment because of a stoppage of work "due to an industrial dispute at the place of his employment". The term "industrial dispute" is explained in Chapter 8. Thus not only the strikers, but those laid off in the same factory or other workplace, are disqualified. However, the Act goes on to permit such persons to "re-qualify", as it were, by showing all of the following:

(*a*) they were not participating in the industrial dispute;
(*b*) they were not financing the industrial dispute;
(*c*) they were not "directly interested" in the industrial dispute; *and*
(*d*) they did not belong to the same "grade or class" as workers who *were* participating in, financing, or directly interested in the industrial dispute.

This places a substantial burden of proof on the applicant. The provisions have been subject to a certain amount of criticism and the Donovan Commission were unanimously of the opinion that the "grade or class" rule, perhaps the most difficult hurdle of all to get over, should be abolished. Nothing has been done to implement this recommendation, however.

There is no reason in principle why the wife and family of the striker should be deprived of social security benefits simply because the breadwinner is taking part in industrial action. Supplementary benefit (which used to be called National Assistance) is available to them on the basis of need alone. But great care is taken to ensure that the striker does not indirectly benefit. Not only are his needs disregarded but, by the Social Security Act 1971, any income he might get during the strike (*e.g.* accrued pay, strike benefit from a union, income tax rebates) must be taken into account in fixing the amount of supplementary benefit. The same Act also put an end to the practice whereby a returning striker, instead of asking for a "sub", or an advance on wages, which was taxable, from his employer, would apply for, and receive, supplementary benefit. Such sums are now recoverable from him, through his employer.

Certain other general disqualifications exist. Those in prison and those who, without good cause, apply for benefit too late are not entitled to unemployment benefit.

IV INDUSTRIAL INJURIES

Only persons in "insurable employment" are entitled to industrial injury benefits. The definition begins with the ordinary contract of service, but contains several extensions to include apprentices, those employed on ships, employees of local authorities and others. The scheme insures them against two risks:

1   Personal injury caused by an accident arising out of and in the course of employment; and
2   Prescribed industrial diseases.

The first risk is hallowed (if that be the right word) by time, being exactly similar to the phrase used in the Workmen's Compensation Acts. The second was introduced to remedy an obvious defect in the first, as will become apparent. Unfortunately, each word in the main definition has been subjected to searching legalistic scrutiny.

Personal Injury

It seems likely that this includes mental as well as physical injuries, though the line may well be drawn at more generalised consequences of stress. The present Act includes disfigurement as a "loss of faculty" (see p. 65), which indirectly supports the view.

Accident

An accident is usually defined in terms of its being unintended or unexpected. But this is unintended or unexpected with regard to the claimant, and so includes acts of nature (*e.g.* frostbite) and malicious acts of third parties (*e.g.* murder). Suicide inevitably causes problems.

> A miner had received injuries at work from which he suffered great pain and was almost blinded. He gassed himself and his widow was granted death benefit on the grounds that the original accident had unhinged him and that provided the causal link between the original accident and the suicide (C.I. 172/50). It is almost impossible to distinguish this case from that of the man who committed suicide after brooding on a doctor's decision that he must stay away from work for a longer period (C.I. 256/49). Perhaps the continual pain makes the difference.

Straightforward, intentional suicide cannot, of course, be an accident.

The main difficulty arising out of the use of the word "accident" has proved to be the problem of distinguishing between injury suffered as a result of accident and that suffered as a result of a "process". "Accident" seems to imply a single indentifiable incident: a "one-off". But many cases of personal injury arise from a process of attrition rather than a sudden stroke of events. A good example among many is the gradual deterioration of hearing that can result from long-term exposure to noises which, though loud, are not loud enough to cause traumatic deafness.

The problem is severe and has tied the tribunals in knots:

> "The question of whether a series of incidents should be regarded as falling within the category of accident or within that of process depends upon the comparative continuity of the incidents constituting the series rather than the duration of the whole series." (C.I. 83/50.)

Perhaps the best approach is to ask whether the alleged "process" can be resolved into a series of "accidents" any one of which could be shown to have caused the injury at that particular moment (even though earlier "accidents" may have predisposed the worker to the type of injury ultimately suffered). If it can, it is an "accident" not a "process". So a nurse who contracted polio seven days after a child she had nursed was held to have suffered an accident, but a doctor who contracted tuberculosis due to continual exposure to infection was not. Despite the quotation above, it also seems that a "process" may in some cases be so short that it can be regarded as an "accident"—*e.g.* when a lorry-driver drove all morning with a broken window and contracted fibrositis.

Out of and in the Course of Employment

Under the old Workmen's Compensation Acts, the worker had to prove both that the accident arose in the course of employment and that it arose "out of" it. The first is not too difficult. The question is similar to that arising in the law of vicarious liability discussed at p. 141. The second is much harder: the employment has, in some sense, to cause the accident. Since 1946 the law provides that if the claimant proves that the accident arose in the course of employment, it is presumed that it arose out of employment unless the contrary is proved (National Insurance (Industrial Injuries) Act 1965, s. 6). Except in the case of accident occurring when the worker was performing totally unauthorised acts, or some cases of "Act of God", such proof of the negative is rarely offered.

Most cases give rise to few problems: industrial accidents usually happen during working hours at the place of work. Peripheral cases do sometimes occur, however. Accidents while the worker is travelling to and from work are specially dealt with by the Act (National Insurance (Industrial Injuries) Act 1965, s. 8). Such accidents will qualify so long as the worker was travelling in a vehicle operated by, or by arrangement with, his employer and not as ordinary public transport, the worker being treated, for the purpose of this part of the

Act, as being *required* as part of his employment so to travel. Other cases are really examples of careful scrutiny of the facts in search of an answer to the question "what was the worker doing?" If he was doing things directly connected with the obligations of his employment, he may claim. But some cases seem to produce surprising results, even so.

> Mr. Culverwell was entitled to a ten-minute tea-break. Smoking was not permitted in the workshop and smoking booths were provided outside. They were nearly always full and workers would squat in the passage waiting for room. While he was doing this, Mr. Culverwell was run over by a fork-lift truck. The time was five minutes after the official end of the tea-break. He was not entitled.
>
> *R. v. Industrial Injuries Commissioner, ex parte AEU* (1966) CA

Prescribed Industrial Diseases

It can be seen that the above definition of an industrial accident, particularly the interpretation of the word "accident" so as to exclude "process", makes it very hard to set up a claim in respect of industrial disease. This is remedied in the Act by prescribing certain types of well-known industrial diseases, generally varieties of pneumoconiosis, in respect of certain employments which commonly give rise to them. A worker who contracts a prescribed industrial disease while so employed is treated as if he had suffered an "accident arising out of and in the course of employment". It should, of course, be pointed out that it is not impossible to make a claim in respect of a disease which is *not* a prescribed industrial disease, merely difficult.

V   INDUSTRIAL INJURY BENEFITS

There are three types of benefit (National Insurance (Industrial Injuries) Act 1965, s. 5). They are: industrial injury benefit (s. 11); industrial disablement benefit (s. 12); industrial death benefit (s. 19).

Industrial Injury Benefit

A worker who is incapable of work as a result of an industrial injury or prescribed disease is entitled to a maximum of 156 days (*i.e.* 26 weeks, Sundays disregarded) of injury benefit. The rates are higher than sickness benefit. No benefit is paid for the first three days unless the worker is away from work for at least 12 days. The only test is incapacity to work: ". . . inability to earn wages or full wages as the case may be at the work at which the injured workman was employed at the time of the accident" (Lord Macnaghten in *Ball* v. *William Hunt and Co. Ltd.* (1912) HL).

Industrial Disablement Benefit

If, at the end of the period of injury benefit, the worker is suffering from a loss of physical or mental faculty assessed at not less than one per cent he is entitled to disablement benefit. If the loss is assessed at 20 per cent or less, benefit is paid as a lump sum, and if more, as a weekly pension. Schedule 3 of the Act lays down an elaborate scheme for assessing disablement as a percentage—*e.g.* loss of a hand or foot, 100 per cent; four fingers of either hand, 50 per cent; small toe, three per cent. This is completely arbitrary and bears no necessary relation to ability to work.

Various supplements (*e.g.* unemployability supplement, hardship allowance, dependants' allowance, constant attendance allowance) may be added to the pension.

Death Benefit

Death benefit is payable to widows, who receive a weekly pension which ceases on remarriage; widowers, if they were incapable of self-support and dependent upon the deceased, who receive a pension for life; and parents, if they can show financial dependence on the deceased.

Benefits may be limited or reduced. There is a maximum for those who are unfortunate enough to suffer successive accidents. Benefits are not payable to those abroad or in prison. Recipients may be disqualified for behaviour likely to retard recovery.

VI ADMINISTRATION AND TRIBUNALS

One of the 1946 reforms was to take national insurance matters away from the courts and give them to officials and tribunals. The structure of the system is complicated, but since the National Insurance Act 1966 the administrations of the National Insurance Act and the National Insurance (Industrial Injuries) Act have been integrated.

In the first instance, claims are determined by the local Insurance Officer. Appeals from his decision go to a local Appeals Tribunal, or, if they are medical cases, to a local Medical Board. These bodies are independent and expert and their function is to decide what is in effect a dispute between the Insurance Officer and the claimant. Appeals from local tribunals in general matters go to the National Insurance Commissioner who may deal with it individually, either himself or though one of his deputies, or, in difficult cases, call a tribunal of Commissioners. Appeals from local Medical Boards go to a Medical Appeal Tribunal whence, in certain cases, it is possible to appeal further to the Commissioner. The decisions of the Commissioners may be reviewed, on a point of law, by proceedings in the High Court.

Certain special questions which may arise under the scheme are reserved to the Minister. If these questions appear in any of the proceedings before Insurance Officers, tribunals, boards or Commissioners then they must be referred to the Minister, who may deal with it himself, appoint an enquiry or refer it to the High Court undetermined. If the Minister does decide, there is an appeal from his decision, on a point of law, to the High Court, whose decision in this instance is final. The reserved questions are oddly varied:

1 Whether enough contributions have been paid to entitle a claimant to benefit.
2 Disputes as to which of several persons are entitled to a benefit that can only be paid to one of them.
3 Which class a person belongs to.
4 Who is to be recognised as maintaining a child.

The procedures are not simple. They are supplemented by regulations and circulars which "oil the wheels". Perhaps one unfortunate aspect is that, despite the elaboration of what was conceived of as an attempt to remove these matters from the jurisdiction of the ordinary courts, the courts still exercise an ultimate supervision, which can make for very protracted litigation.

Chapter 5

Trade Unions

I   REGISTERED AND UNREGISTERED TRADE UNIONS

When trade unions were first formed, they were formed as simple members' clubs: in law, they were not legal persons but simply a set of agreements between the members in terms of the rule-book. And to begin with, they were illegal. Gradually, this illegality was removed until, by the Trade Union Act 1871, they were recognised as lawful organisations. In the meantime, however, other types of associations which had not had the problem of illegality had been granted more than recognition. The law had stepped in to provide some solution to the practical difficulties of preserving their property and money which arose from their cumbrous legal nature. These benefits were generally accorded by way of registration.

So the Trade Union Act 1871 provided a system of registration for trade unions. There were virtually no conditions attached—it was simply an option given to unions—and the benefits, though small, were worth having. Most trade unions registered and gained the advantage of the new means of protecting their property and interests.

The framers of the Industrial Relations Act saw another purpose in registration. It could be used as part of a general campaign to ensure that trade unions did not behave badly towards their members and conducted their affairs in a fair and reasonable manner. The Registrar was given a supervisory role and unions were encouraged to register by means of a simple stick and carrot approach:

Registered	Unregistered
Described as "trade union" in the Act.	Described as "organisation of workers" in the Act, though not the Code.
Tax benefits for provident funds (Income and Corporation Taxes Act 1970, s. 338).	Benefits only obtainable in respect of separate provident society.
Employees have an enforceable right to join or not to join and to take part in activities (Industrial Relations Act, s. 5).	Employees only have the enforceable right *not* to join.
May enter Agency Shop or Approved Closed Shop agreements.	May not.
May initiate Sole Bargaining Agency procedure and may be appointed Sole Bargaining Agent.	May not: though may be involved in discussions initiated by others.
May initiate procedure agreement enquiry.	May not: though may be involved in discussions initiated by others.
Not liable under s. 96 (inducing breach of contract—see Chapter 8).	Liable.
Officials (including stewards) are in general protected from personal liability while acting on behalf of the union.	Not protected.
Limitation on amount of compensation which may be awarded against union under Act.	No limit.
Right to report claims under s. 8 of the Terms and Conditions of Employment Act 1959.	No right.

There are other matters: these are the most important. However, most large trade unions, in pursuance of the policy worked out at the TUC, have not registered and prefer to weather the disadvantages for the benefit of being exempt from the supervision of the Registrar.

As mentioned above, in strictness the term "trade union" should be reserved for a union registered under the Act. This does not accord with common usage and in this book we shall follow the example set in the Code of Industrial Relations Practice and use the terms "registered trade union" and "unregistered trade union". The definition of a trade union is not complicated: an organisation, temporary or permanent, consisting "wholly or mainly" of workers "of one or more descriptions", whose principal objects include the regulations of relations between workers of that description and employers (Industrial Relations Act, s. 61). An organisation must, therefore, have ordinary trade union activities (collective bargaining, etc.) among its main objects and must open its membership to workers within a "description"—though there is no apparent limit to the breadth of such a description. Before the Act, trade unions were not defined in terms of membership in this way, and many employers' associations, as a result, came within the definition. Under the Act, employers' associations are dealt with by parallel and roughly equivalent provisions. But these provisions are of no great practical importance and will not be considered in detail in this book.

The standard method of registration is by simple application to the Registrar, together with a copy of the rules, names and addresses of the branches, a report of the previous year's activities and the appropriate fee. If the Registrar is satisfied that the union is both independent and has power to alter its rules and deal with its property without interference by another body, he must register the organisation as a trade union (s. 67). There are special provisions for federations.

When the Act came into force, however, registration was put into operation by means of a provisional register, upon which were entered the names of all trade unions (the majority) that had been registered under the old 1871 Trade Union Act. The Registrar was empowered to transfer such unions to the permanent register without the union making any application at all (ss. 78–79). Thus unions not wishing to be registered had positively to de-register. This is a simple matter, involving only a request to the Registrar (s. 92(1) (a)), the only problem being that unions whose rules require them to be registered had to change those rules before the Registrar could be satisfied that it was, in truth, the *union* that was requesting de-registration.

The general results of registration have been outlined above and will become obvious in other parts of this book. The Act clearly discriminates in very many places in favour of the registered union. But that is not the only consequence. Once a union is registered it becomes subject to the supervisory powers of the Registrar. This is not to say that unregistered unions are totally free of supervision, but the supervision that is common to registered and unregistered unions is mainly connected with the protection of members, and will be dealt with in the next chapter.

"As soon as practicable" after registration, the Registrar examines the rule-book of the union (s. 75). He has two purposes. The rules must not be inconsistent with the "guiding principles" that are set out in s. 65 of the Act. These are binding upon all unions, registered or unregistered, and are concerned with the rights of members. They are dealt with in detail in Chapter 6. For our present purposes, it should be noted that these principles, in general, require fair treatment of members. For instance, a member subjected to disciplinary procedure has a right to a "full and fair hearing". So the Registrar, when he reads the rule-book, is concerned to see that the rules set up a system which can be operated fairly in the interests of members.

The rule-book must comply with the requirements of Schedule 4 of the Act. This schedule, which applies only to registered unions, sets out a number of basic necessities for what might be regarded as the good and efficient administration of the union. The rules must:

> Specify the name, address and objects of the union;
> Define the relationship between the branches and the
>   central organisation;

Provide for the election of a governing body;

Set out the way in which members of the governing body
may be removed;

Provide for the election or appointment of officers, and
their removal;

If there are other types of official (e.g. shop stewards),
provide similarly for them;

Specify the powers and duties of the governing body,
officers and officials;

Set out the procedure for meetings;

Specify how the rules may be changed;

Specify who may give instructions for industrial action;

Set out how ballots and elections are to be run;

Provide for the winding-up of the union;

Define who is eligible for membership and how applications are to be handled;

Specify dues and the procedure on non-payment;

In respect of discipline, define the behaviour in question,
the penalties and the procedure;

Set out procedures for other sorts of termination of membership;

Set out a complaints procedure;

Specify how the property may be used and benefits distributed, including distribution of assets on winding-up;

Provide for the keeping of accounts and audit.

Some of these matters are covered elsewhere in the Act (regular audit, for example) and most would be regarded as ordinary
provisions that any union that wanted to run itself efficiently
would have.

If the Registrar is not satisfied that the rule-book is consis-
tent with the guiding principles and complies with Schedule
4, he has power to require the union to alter its rules. The
ultimate sanction is cancellation of registration (which does
not seem severe in the present climate of opinion), which may
be ordered by NIRC on the application of the Registrar (s. 76).
In addition, the Registrar may apply to NIRC for cancellation
of registration on other grounds: that the registration was
obtained by fraud or mistake; that the organisation has ceased

to be an independent trade union; that the union has defaulted in its "administrative" obligations (see below).

Apart from this, the Registrar has a general supervisory jurisdiction in respect of the guiding principles and the rules (ss. 81–83). This may be activated in two ways. An individual aggrieved by a breach of the rules or a disregard of the guiding principles by a registered union may complain to the Registrar, who may investigate. He may be able to promote a settlement, but failing that, he may refer the complaint to an industrial tribunal, even when the individual in question has second thoughts and is unwilling to take the matter further (s. 108). In serious cases, the matter may go to NIRC (s. 103) who have the power of issuing mandatory orders to the union. Clearly this is more than using public resources to assist injured individuals, the Registrar is conducting a public investigation.

Additionally, if the Registrar "has reason to suspect" that there has been a *serious* breach of the rules or guiding principles, or *persistent* breaches, he may investigate on his own initiative. This investigation may end with the Registrar seeking an undertaking from the union: if this is not forthcoming, the matter is referred to NIRC who may make an order in the same terms (s. 104). These investigatory powers clearly give strong "teeth" to the supervision of registered unions.

Finally, registered unions are subject to the "administrative provisions" contained in ss. 87–91 of the Act. These require registered unions to:

> Keep proper accounts;
> Maintain a register of members;
> Submit an annual return and audit to the Registrar;
> Distribute an annual report of its activities to its members, which will include the Registrar's return and audit;
> Submit any superannuation scheme to an actuary for report;
> Report all changes of rules, addresses and officers to the Registrar.

This is one of the few parts of the Act where old-fashioned criminal sanctions are used. It is an offence, punishable by a fine of £100, wilfully to neglect to perform any of these duties: wilful falsification of documents in this connection is punishable by a fine of £400 (s. 91).

The Registrar also has power to initiate the winding-up of an insolvent registered union (s. 90).

Registered unions are, in law, corporate bodies as soon as they are registered: they are legal persons and hold their own property and may sue or be sued in their registered name (s. 74). Unregistered unions, on the other hand, must continue to hold their property through trustees (as all unions did before the Act). However, by virtue of s. 154, unregistered unions may sue and be sued in their own name so the lack of corporate personality, though a nuisance, does not give them any immunity or disadvantage in legal proceedings.

II POLITICAL ACTIVITIES

Trade unions have engaged in political activities for over a 100 years. However, in 1910, a trade union member who disagreed with the use of union funds to support Labour Members of Parliament brought proceedings alleging that such expenditure was illegal, since it was not mentioned as a trade union activity in the Trade Union Act of 1871. The House of Lords held in his favour (*ASRS* v. *Osborne* (1910) HL). The result was the Trade Union Act 1913 which on the one hand made it clear that political activity was perfectly lawful for trade unions, and on the other imposed a degree of complicated control over the use of union funds for such activities. The Act is still largely with us.

The Act applies to all unions, registered or not, insofar as they use money in the support of candidates at parliamentary or local elections, the maintenance of M.P.s and other public officers, the holding of political meetings, the distribution of political literature, and other supporting activities. Such a union must adopt a code of rules which sets up a separate political fund and provide for its control: these rules must satisfy the Registrar and model rules are available. Members who do not wish to contribute to the political fund must be allowed to "contract out" and all members must be informed of their rights. A "contracted out" member must not be placed under any disadvantage within the union, save only as regards the management of the political fund itself.

It should be emphasised that there is no sort of control over the general political activities of trade unions or their members, merely over the use of general union funds for certain specified purposes. Furthermore, the holding of meetings or the distribution of literature which is mainly for the "trade union" purposes of the union may be paid for from general funds even if it is also a political activity.

Chapter 6

Membership of Trade Unions

I UNION MEMBERSHIP AND THE CLOSED SHOP

The right to belong or not to belong to a trade union is rarely a simple matter of an individual and an organisation. It usually involves the man's employment, and therefore his employer, and may also be regarded as a matter of public concern justifying public intervention.

It was estimated that in 1964 some $3\frac{3}{4}$ million workers (out of $22\frac{3}{4}$ million) worked in closed shops, some $\frac{3}{4}$ million being in "pre-entry" closed shops (see the Donovan Report, Chapter XI). By "pre-entry" closed shop is meant the system whereby a worker cannot get a job unless he is already a member of a given union, while "post-entry" denotes the situation where a man is taken on on condition that he joins the union later. Other systems exist, such as the "employment agency" system, where the union plays a part (great or small) in the selection of employees for an employer, and the "preference" system, whereby an employer agrees to give preference to qualified union members over non-unionists in filling vacancies.

Without abuse, many find much to commend closed shop systems: it can make for stability and discipline in industrial relations and it clearly strengthens the position of trade unions. Abuses may occur, such as when a man is arbitrarily refused membership of a union, or arbitrarily expelled from membership. The objections to closed shops, however, are not in the main cast in terms of abuses or of practical problems of industrial relations, but in general principle and political tenet. It is said to be wrong to force a man to join what is essentially a voluntary organisation as a price for giving him a job: it is said to be wrong to allow unions to interfere with the employer's prerogative of hiring and firing. Possibly such arguments could be countered by others based on a less individualistic view of society, but equally political in nature. The point is that the approach of any legislation to the question of trade union membership is likely to be coloured by political assumption.

The Industrial Relations Act declares war on the closed shop—but not total war. The closed shop is not declared illegal and is not really outlawed. It may still be practised (and clearly is), but at a cost. The cost is that certain rights accorded to workers against employers, to employers against unions and to individuals against unions may be infringed. And if they are infringed certain consequences, generally the payment of compensation, may ensue.

II THE WORKER AND HIS EMPLOYER: SECTION 5

Section 5 of the Act lays down that "every worker shall, as between himself and his employer" have three rights. These are:

(a) The right to be a member of such registered trade union as he may choose.

(b) The right to refuse to be a member of any trade union (registered or unregistered) at all, or of any particular union. This right is subject to the "agency shop" and "approved closed shop" exceptions.

(c) The right to take part in the activities of a registered union at an "appropriate time", and the right to stand for and hold office in the registered union.

The rights as to union membership are reasonably straightforward—of course, the built-in bias towards registered unions in the circumstances of massive refusal to register has given the operation of this part of s. 5 a peculiarly lop-sided look.

The right to participate in union activities is less clear. It is not only limited by being confined to the activities of registered unions, the activities must take place at an "appropriate time". This is further defined in s. 5(5) as either some time outside working hours or some time inside working hours in accordance with arrangements agreed with the employer or consent given by him.

In a complicated piece of litigation concerning the rights of members and officials of the TSA, a registered union organising telephonists, not recognised by the Post Office, the point was raised that, since the section nowhere mentioned *where* these activities were to take place, it could not be assumed that members were to exercise their rights on the employer's premises. That would be to derogate from *his* rights of property. Although this argument found in favour in NIRC, it was unanimously rejected in the Court of Appeal. Members and officials of registered trade unions could carry on with union activities (at least, those of the "organisational" kind—see below) when they were lawfully on the premises outside working hours, *i.e.* before and after work and during breaks (*Crouch* v. *Post Office* (1973) CA; under appeal to the House of Lords at time of writing). Clearly, there is much here that could give rise to argument, and, given the industrial relations background of cases such as this, the points will not easily be settled.

Section 5 rights belong to the worker and are exercisable against the employer. The employer, the section goes on to say, must not do any of three things:

(a) Prevent or deter the worker from exercising his rights.
(b) Dismiss, penalise or otherwise discriminate against him for exercising his rights.
(c) Subject to Agency Shops and Approved Closed Shops, refuse to take a man on because he was a member of a registered union or because he was not a member of a union, registered or unregistered.

In practice, these resolve themselves into three situations:

(i)—*Dismissal*

Dismissal for exercising or threatening to exercise a s. 5 right is, as we saw in Chapter 3, always unfair. The only problem is proof. Further, because of the wide discretion a tribunal has, the narrow limits of s. 5 rights can to some extent be disregarded: dismissals may be unfair even where, technically, no right was infringed. The individual will be compensated and may receive a recommendation for reinstatement. There is no two-year qualifying period for s. 5 claims.

(ii)—*Refusal to engage*

This, in practice, will be much more difficult. If an employer operates a policy of excluding non-unionists he is most unlikely to declare the fact. Assuming the case can be proved, the individual may complain to the local industrial tribunal and may receive compensation. But in this case, unlike dismissal, the tribunal has no power to recommend reinstatement, which would not be appropriate (s. 106).

(iii)—*Discrimination, deterrence, penalties*

This is very broad. In fact, the Act goes so far as to declare that if an employer "without any suggestion of reward for compliance or penalty for non-compliance, seeks to encourage the worker to join a (registered) trade union which the employer recognises as having negotiating rights in respect of him", this shall not constitute prevention or deterrence. Which leads to the perhaps unjustified conclusion that everything else may be. Certainly, benefits, bonuses, promotions, access to overtime, etc., must all be distributed without regard to union affiliation or activities. Otherwise, the individual may claim compensation before the industrial tribunal.

The TSA case also raised the question of how far discrimination against the *union*, which the employer was entitled to do, being perfectly free to recognise and negotiate with the unregistered UPOW if he chose, counted as discrimination against the members. NIRC was clear that it did not—except where it directly affected individual members, *e.g.* where the Post Office delivered UPOW letters to members, but not TSA letters; or where UPOW members were allowed representation by union officials in disciplinary matters, but TSA members were not. The Court of Appeal went further, the Master of the Rolls (Lord Denning) saying roundly that discrimination against the union was discrimination against all its members. However, the majority of the Court distinguished between *negotiating* matters, where the Post Office could legitimately discriminate, and *organisational* matters, such as recruitment, collecting subscriptions, entertaining officials, etc. ("the life-blood of the union"), which would involve discrimination between members and so be impermissible. As mentioned earlier, the case is still under appeal at time of writing: *any* line drawn in this matter is likely to cause difficulties.

Section 5 rights are exercisable only against the employer. The claims under this section are treated almost exactly similarly to claims for unfair dismissal under s. 22. Further, in s. 33, the Act specifically states that no account is to be taken of any pressure put on the employer by way of industrial action. "Industrial action" is industrial action as defined by the Act: a strike or threat of a strike, or "irregular industrial action short of a strike" or a threat of it. These terms are further described in Chapter 7. Nor is such pressure to be taken into account in assessing compensation (s. 116(5)). The employer must "carry the can" and pay the compensation, assessed, presumably, on criteria similar to those used in unfair dismissal (see p. 54) and subject to the overall limit of £4,160 or two years' pay, whichever is the less (s. 118).

III   THE EMPLOYER AND THE UNION

The first thing the Act does here is to declare agreements for pre-entry closed shops (including "employment agency" agreements) to be "void". An individual who thinks he has been refused employment because of the existence of a pre-entry closed shop agreement may apply to NIRC to have the agreement (if found to exist) formally declared void. "Void" means without legal effect. Such an agreement would in any case be a collective agreement, whose binding force is conferred by s. 34 of the Act, which permits the parties to deprive it of legal effect by an appropriately worded clause. Most collective agreements are so equipped. So the sanction of "voidness" has little practical force.

But the employer, who, as we have seen, must carry the can for discriminating against non-trade unionists, or against trade unionists, even if he acts in execution of a policy agreed with, or forced on him by, a trade union, is given certain rights himself. Under s. 33, if industrial action has been taken or threatened to make him infringe a s. 5 right, or to keep to a void pre-entry closed-shop agreement, this constitutes an unfair industrial practice and the employer may take proceedings before NIRC, which may lead to compensation or "desist orders" (see Chapter 8). Section 105 makes it clear (in rather obscure language) that only the employer may make such a complaint to NIRC, a point that had to be elucidated in *Langston* v. *AEWU* (1973) NIRC.

IV AGENCY SHOPS AND APPROVED CLOSED SHOPS

The net result so far might be said to make closed shops possible only on the terms that employers should be willing to pay occasional sums in compensation to those who could show that they had been refused employment or discriminated against. The Act, however, offers a general alternative to a closed shop—the Agency Shop.

An Agency Shop is constituted by agreement between an employer and a *registered* trade union. It is not open to unregistered unions. It applies to a unit of workers (here called "workers of one or more descriptions") and provides that they shall all be employed on the condition that they are (or become) members of that registered union or pay "appropriate contributions" (s. 11). Once the agreement is made, a worker loses his right to refuse to be a member of that trade union. Consequently he has no complaint against his employer if he has been dismissed, penalised or discriminated against for not being a member of that union, or has been refused employment because he is not a member and refuses to join (s. 6). Such a worker does, however, have the alternative right to pay "appropriate contributions" and not join. Appropriate contributions are defined by the agreement, but must not exceed the union subscriptions (excluding the political fund dues) (s. 8). If he objects on grounds of conscience both to being a member and to paying appropriate contributions he may propose to the union that he pay the sums (here called "equivalent contributions") to charity. In default of agreement, either as to grounds or the charity, the matter is referred to an industrial tribunal for settlement (ss. 9, 10). Outside the well-established cases of certain religious sects, it is hard to see how these conscience provisions will be put into effect.

If an employer refuses to agree to an Agency Shop, a registered union, provided that it is recognised by the employer as having negotiating rights for the workers in question, may apply to NIRC for a *compulsory* Agency Shop. The matter is referred by NIRC to the CIR to conduct a ballot among the workers in question (s. 12). The CIR has a discretion as to the definition of the unit of workers concerned and may report back to NIRC that the unit as originally defined should be amended. If a majority of those entitled to vote, or two-thirds of those voting, are in favour, then the employer must enter into an Agency Shop agreement and carry it out. These duties may be enforced by NIRC by mandatory order (s. 102) and it is an unfair industrial practice to take industrial action to prevent the employer from carrying them out. If, on the other hand, the required majority in favour is not obtained, then NIRC makes an order that no Agency Shop, voluntary or compulsory, shall be made between that employer and that union in respect of that unit of workers for two years (s. 13(3)).

A compulsory Agency Shop must stand for two years, but after that time (and, in the case of voluntary Agency Shops, at any time) if one-fifth of the workers in the unit make a requisition in writing to NIRC, a ballot is organised by the CIR on the continuance of the Agency Shop. If a majority of the unit, or two-thirds of those voting, do not vote in favour of its continuance, the Agency Shop is revoked and a two-year freeze is imposed (s. 15(3)). If the Agency Shop is supported in the ballot, then no further application for its revocation can be entertained for two years (s. 15(4)). It is an unfair industrial practice for employers or unions to take industrial action to interfere with any of these ballots (s. 16).

There is nothing to prevent an Agency Shop agreement, whether it be voluntary or compulsory, being voluntarily abandoned by agreement between the employer and union concerned.

Although, because of the political events surrounding the Industrial Relations Act, the use of the Agency Shop has not been as widespread as might have been expected, these provisions of the Act have been used to a certain extent.

An Agency Shop has two categories of worker within it who are not members of the union—the "contributing non-members" who pay "appropriate contributions" and the "conscience men" who pay "equivalent contributions" to charity. Despite the obscurity of the wording of the provisions of the Act, the second category is not likely to be large and would not be expected, therefore, to cause much difficulty. Contributing non-members pose different problems. They do not have to go through any procedure to put themselves in that category: they have an absolute right to be there at their option. They are not subject to union discipline and may, indeed, be members of other, rival, organisations at the same time. In industries where the closed shop has become an integral part of the system of hiring and employment, such a group could not easily be fitted in. Accordingly representations were made, particularly by the shipping industry and the National Union of Seamen, and by Equity, the actors' union, that some exception should be made to deal with such problems. The Bill was amended in its passage through Parliament and the Approved Closed Shop was born (ss. 17, 18; Sch. 1).

The Approved Close Shop is essentially an Agency Shop without the contributing non-members. Within three months (or one month, if he is a new employee) each worker in the unit must either join the union or make his "conscience" proposal, as in an Agency Shop. Like an Agency Shop, the Approved Closed Shop agreement may only be made by a registered union, but unlike it, it only comes into effect after

a full investigation by the CIR initiated by a *joint* application to NIRC. During that investigation, the proposed
agreement must surmount five separate hurdles—all very high
ones :

1   It must be necessary to enable the workers to be
    organised as representative, responsible and effective
    bodies for bargaining.
2   It must be necessary to maintain reasonable terms
    and conditions of employment and reasonable pros-
    pects of continued employment.
3   It must be necessary to promote or maintain stable
    collective bargaining arrangements.
4   It must be necessary to prevent collective agreements
    from being frustrated.
5   It must be shown that the first four requirements
    could not be met by an Agency Shop.

Only when these hurdles are surmounted is a ballot held, and
even then only if one-fifth of the workers request it in writing.
The majorities required are the same as in Agency Shops.
If the ballot does not approve the agreement, then it does not
come into effect and there is a two-year freeze. There are
provisions for ballots as to continuance similar to those for
Agency Shops. If the agreement is approved, there is no statutory obligation on an employer to carry it out, as there is in
the case of a compulsory Agency Shop, but, by definition, an
employer must support every Approved Closed Shop since a
joint application is necessary to initiate proceedings.

So far, both the actors and the seamen have successfully
used the procedure. But in both cases, the Approved Closed
Shops will only continue so long as the unions remain on the
register.

V   THE WORKER AND THE UNION:
THE CONTRACT OF MEMBERSHIP

The third side of the legal triangle created by union membership is the line which connects the union with the indivi-

dual worker. Here the question is much wider than that of the closed shop: it includes fair treatment as a member, equal opportunity within the union and such matters, as well as discipline, expulsion and the right to join.

As was mentioned in the last chapter, a trade union in law is basically the sum of the contracts made by the members when they join. This is still a dominant factor, even when the union, by registration, has obtained legal personality. The rights and duties of members, officers and officials of the union are primarily decided by the contract of membership. And the terms of the contract of membership are found in the union rule-book and nowhere else.

> Mr. Spring was recruited by the National Amalgamated Stevedores and Dockers Society without having first cleared his arrears of subscriptions with the TGWU. The TGWU made a complaint to the Disputes Committee of the TUC, which ordered the NASDS to expel Mr. Spring and other members like him. This was done. The NASDS has no rule permitting expulsion on such grounds and Mr. Spring successfully sued them.
>
> *Spring* v. *NASDS* (1956) Lanc Pal Ct

Apart from the provisions of Schedule 4 of the Industrial Relations Act which apply only to registered unions, and the Trade Union Act 1913, which regulates political funds, there are no legal requirements as to the contents of the rule-book. Union rules may deal with any matter they choose as the union thinks fit. The law simply requires that the rules be observed. But, especially in matters concerning the rights of individual members, the courts can be very searching in their analysis of the rules.

> Lee and Shaw were both travelling showmen and members of the Showmen's Guild, a trade union. They had a dispute as to which was entitled, under the union rules, to occupy No. 2 site at Bradford Summer Fair. The union decided in favour of Shaw, but Lee occupied the site. Shaw complained to the Area Committee who

exercised their power under the rules to fine for "unfair competition" and imposed a fine of £100. Lee did not pay. Under the rules, if fines were not paid within a month, the member was "deemed to have resigned". The committee decided Lee was not a member. The Court of Appeal, however, issued a declaration that the expulsion was void since Lee was not truly guilty of unfair competition on the Court's analysis of the rule, and therefore the fine was void and his expulsion with it.

Lee v. *Showmen's Guild of Great Britain* (1952) CA

The courts have also been prepared to go beyond this by applying the idea of "natural justice" to decisions taken within unions which affect members. Most cases have been cases of expulsion, but the principle is of wider application. In essence the "rules of natural justice" require that a person be given a fair hearing, with an opportunity to state his side of the case before an unbiased "tribunal". A fair hearing does not necessarily mean an independent hearing—in the nature of things it will be a union body that will decide in a dispute between a member and a union—but does mean that no bias must be shown. Nor is there a right to cross-examine, merely a right to have the "other side" of the case stated. It is still not precisely clear *when* the duty to obey the rules of natural justice will be imposed by the courts. Two approaches have been adopted: when it is possible to imply such a duty into the rule as a matter of construction (see *per* Maugham, J., in *Maclean* v. *Workers' Union* (1929) ChD); and whenever a decision is made which affects a man's property or position (see Ungoed-Thomas, J., in *Lawlor* v. *UPOW* (1965) ChD). There is also the subsidiary question of whether natural justice can be excluded by, for example, a union rule which clearly grants the right to reach an arbitrary, discretionary decision: some judges, notably Lord Denning, firmly deny this (see *Breen* v. *AEU* (1971) CA). But it is fair to say that the courts have shown a very great willingness to apply these ideas to trade unions when they are disciplining their members. Moreover, they have been prepared to grant not only declarations of legal rights, but injunctions requiring wrongfully expelled members not to be excluded from the union, and have awarded damages. The following cases may serve as examples:

> Maclean was a member of the Executive Committee of the Workers' Union and had a long-standing dispute with other members. He ran for President of the union. In that connection, he issued a circular without permission, which was a breach of the rules, punishable primarily by a fine of 2s. 6d., but also by expulsion if the Executive Committee thought fit. The Executive Committee considered the case and Maclean was present and spoke on his own behalf. He was expelled. The Court held that there had been no breach of natural justice: he had had a hearing and no open bias had been shown.
>
> *Maclean* v. *Workers' Union* (1929) ChD

> Bonsor was a professional musician. He fell into arrears with his subscriptions, which rendered him liable to expulsion by the Branch Committee. He was expelled by the Branch Secretary. He was unable to work as a musician for five years. The House of Lords awarded him a declaration that he was still a member and an injunction preventing the union from excluding him from membership and also substantial damages for the loss he had suffered through being unemployed.
>
> *Bonsor* v. *Musicians' Union* (1955) HL

> Lawlor was expelled from the UPOW without being given notice of the charge nor an opportunity to state a case to the Executive Council. An appeal lay to the union's Annual Meeting. Under the rules the Executive Council had power to expel any person who "in the opinion of the council" was not a "fit and proper person for membership". The Court held the expulsion void, since the rules of natural justice had not been observed (despite the discretionary wording of the rule) and granted relief notwithstanding the fact that Lawlor had

not exercised his internal right to appeal to the annual
meeting, since the Executive Committee had not sus-
pended his expulsion pending his appeal.

Lawlor v. *UPOW* (1965) ChD

Breen was elected shop steward at Fawley Oil Refinery.
By the rules of the AEU his election had to be confirmed
by the District Committee. The District Committee
refused to confirm it, and did not give Breen a hearing.
Breen protested, the matter was reconsidered and a letter
was sent to Breen explaining the Committee's reasons.
By an honest mistake, the letter contained one reason
which was false, but which in fact had not affected the
Committee's decision. The other reason was true and
had been acted on. The Court of Appeal held that there
was a duty to observe the rules of natural justice and
give Breen's case fair consideration, but the Committee
had done so.

Breen v. *AEU* (1971) CA

The contract of membership is something which exists
between a member and a union. It is thus of no value if the
courts are to consider a complaint that the individual was
unfairly refused membership—no contract has ever been
made. Indeed, this has been taken further. If the union's
membership rules do not permit the individual to be a member,
there is no way in which the courts can treat him as one,
even in the case where he has been mistakenly treated as a
member by the union itself. Which can lead to surprising
results:

Faramus joined the Film Artistes' Association in 1950.
Its rules provided that no person who had been convicted
of certain criminal offences should be eligible for membership. In 1958 it was discovered that Faramus had committed such offences, in 1938 and 1940, his last offences
being acts of sabotage against the occupying German
forces in Jersey. The House of Lords held that he never

was a member and was therefore not entitled to relief for the unfair manner of his "expulsion".

Faramus v. *Film Artistes' Association* (1964) HL

VI   THE WORKER AND THE UNION: THE INDUSTRIAL RELATIONS ACT

The Industrial Relations Act did not repeal the common law relating to union membership. It supplemented it in two ways. First, it enacted a code of "guiding principles for the conduct of" trade unions, which are all concerned with the protection of the interests of individual members. Secondly, the Act provided supplementary procedures for enforcing both these and the contractual rights.

All trade unions, registered and unregistered, must observe the guiding principles set out in s. 65. They are:

1   Every person qualified for membership shall have a right to join.
2   Every member shall have a right to resign.
3   Every member shall have the right to be a candidate for, or hold any union office, to nominate candidates, to vote, to attend meetings and participate in them.
4   Voting shall be by secret ballot.
5   Every member shall have a fair opportunity to vote, without interference or constraint.
6   No member shall be subjected to "unfair or unreasonable disciplinary action" and in particular, no member shall be disciplined for:
    (*a*) Refusing to commit an unfair industrial practice;
    (*b*) Refusing to take part in a strike *not* called "in contemplation or furtherance of an industrial dispute" or which constitutes an unfair industrial practice;
    (*c*) Refusing to take part in irregular industrial action short of a strike called in circumstances such as those set out at (*b*) above.

    7   Except in cases of non-payment of subscriptions and dues, if a member is disciplined, he must have:

        (*a*) written notice of the charges and time to prepare his defence;

        (*b*) a full and fair hearing;

        (*c*) written statement of the findings; and

        (*d*) where he has the right to appeal, time to appeal;

    before any disciplinary action is taken against him.

    8   There should be no termination of membership unless the member is given reasonable notice complete with reasons.

    9   No member shall be restrained from taking any form of legal proceeding.

The phrases "unfair industrial practice", "in contemplation or furtherance of an industrial dispute" and "irregular industrial action short of a strike" are explained in Chapter 8.

These principles cover a good deal of ground in some considerable detail. By way of commentary, it ought to be said that the "right" mentioned in principles 1 and 3 is cast in negative form. A member "shall not, by way of any arbitrary or unreasonable discrimination, be excluded from" being a candidate, etc. This gives the union some undefined power to exclude, so long as it is exercised on reasonable, fair grounds. The right to be a member is worth examining further. A union, it will be remembered, is defined as an organisation of workers "of one or more descriptions". Trade unions define their members, naturally enough, in terms of the work they do. The guiding principle says that any person who applies for membership and is within that description and is "appropriately qualified *for employment* as a worker of that description" shall not, by way of any arbitrary or unreasonable discrimination, be refused membership. It is not uncommon for trade unions to have rules which impose conditions of eligibility other than these—*e.g.* that members should have no criminal record, etc. These conditions are disregarded by the guiding principle and the guiding principle is overriding.

The overriding effect of the guiding principles leads on to

more general points. The custom and practice of the union, even the rule-book itself, is no defence for a union accused of having disregarded a guiding principle. Of course, registered unions will have had their rules examined to ensure that there is no obvious clash between them and the principles. In their case the guiding principles will govern the exercise by officials and others of discretion conferred by the rules. But in the case of unregistered unions the rules and the principles may be in direct conflict. An official of an unregistered union may act under a perfectly lawful rule of his union and yet fall foul of the guiding principles.

It can be seen that the guiding principles are wider in application than the common law rules explained in the last section. They apply to non-members seeking membership: Mr. Faramus would have had a claim under the principles. They are detailed, requiring secret ballots, written notices and statements of reasons, for example. They lay down that certain types of disciplinary action are always to be considered unfair or unreasonable. The aim is clearly to provide a detailed code of practice for unions to adopt towards their members.

The Act also provides several new procedures to enforce not only these new rights but the old rights created by the contract of membership. The aim is, no doubt, to transfer this sort of case from the ordinary courts to the new courts and tribunals set up under the Act. But the old law has not been repealed and it is still possible to take ordinary legal proceedings for breach of the rule-book or failure to observe the rules of natural justice. All else is additional.

First, by s. 66, breach of the guiding principles is declared to be an unfair industrial practice. This means that, under s. 101, any person "against whom the action was taken" may apply to NIRC who may make a declaration of rights, an award of compensation, or an order that the union desist in the action, or any combination of all three. Secondly, individual members, persons who have involuntarily ceased to be members, or disappointed applicants may take proceedings before an industrial tribunal either for a breach of the guiding principles or a breach of the rules (or both). These claims (under s. 107) may lead to a declaration or an award of compensation, but *not* a "desist order" (s. 109). Thirdly, if the union is registered, such individuals may apply to the Registrar (s. 81), who will investigate and try to promote a settlement. As we saw in Chapter 5, investigations by the Registrar, whether they are initiated by an individual or begun by the Registrar himself, may end with the Registrar referring the matter to an industrial tribunal (if the individual initiated the investigation) or NIRC (if the Registrar did).

This completes the "membership triangle". Disputes about union membership may lead to complaints by workers against employers under s. 5, complaints by employers against trade unions under s. 33 or to complaints by individuals (or the Registrar) against trade unions under the common law or s. 65.

Chapter 7

Collective Bargaining

I COLLECTIVE AGREEMENTS AND PROCEDURES

Since the desired end of collective bargaining is often a collective agreement, it may seem odd to begin a chapter on collective bargaining with a consideration of collective agreements. But collective agreements have two functions. They set out terms and conditions intended to apply to the employment of those upon whose behalf they are made. The legal question here—the effect of collective agreements upon individual contracts of employment—was discussed in Chapter 2. Their second function is to set up procedures; that is, methods and systems whereby good industrial relations may be promoted, grievances settled and claims dealt with without recourse to industrial action. This, the "public" side of collective agreements, was considered by the authors of the Industrial Relations Act to have great importance.

To this extent, then, collective agreements logically come first. It is by collective agreements that conditions are set for collective bargaining.

The primary legal question about this aspect of collective agreements is whether or not they are "legally enforceable". At first sight, many of them look very much like ordinary contracts. It is true that many do not, of course: the decisions of Joint Industrial Councils or the results of a shop stewards' "meeting with management" can look more like administrative decisions or legislative enactments, but the general point holds good. If this is so, the argument runs, to treat them as enforceable, "just like any other commercial contract", will make for stability and discipline.

There are, of course, difficulties. In practice, we are talking about the enforcement of the "public" side of a collective agreement. If an agreement provides a procedure for dealing with claims, should strike action taken without using the procedure be regarded as a breach of contract? The first difficulty is that, although very many strikes are "unconstitutional" and in breach of procedures, they are also "unofficial" and taken without prior union authorisation. We saw in Chapter 2 that, in law, a union, when bargaining, very rarely acts as the agent of the workers concerned. It acts independently. Therefore, if the collective agreement is a contract, it is a contract between the employer (or the employers' association) and the union. There is a general principle of the law of contract (privity of contract) that C can neither take rights nor incur obligations on a contract made by A and B. So in practice, it would often be very difficult to hold the union, as party to the contract, liable for breach of contract, and always impossible to hold unofficial strikers liable.

There are other arguments, too. It is often asserted (though rarely with convincing examples) that collective agreements are too informal, and not "legal" enough, to constitute contracts. Furthermore, many are so subject to re-negotiation that it may be difficult to say at any given moment whether the agreement is still in force. Arguments such as these, together with the undoubted fact that the civil courts have rarely provided a constructive forum for industrial relations, led many lawyers to take the view that, in general, collective agreements were not enforceable as contracts. They lacked one particular legal requirement—there was no "intent to create legal relations" on the part of the parties to them. The basis of this idea is that agreements which are clearly outside the realm of public enforcement, such as, for example, family arrangements as to housekeeping money or the friendly offer of a lift to work, are not to be enforced in the courts.

In 1969, in *Ford Motor Co.* v. *AEU* (1969) HC, this point of view was accepted. The extent of acceptance was not clear and it is still not possible to be dogmatic about how far any particular collective agreement is legally binding at common law, but very many are not. The Industrial Relations Act, in s. 34, modified this decision by laying down that every collective agreement made in writing after the Act came into force should be treated as legally enforceable unless it contained a clause to the contrary effect (the earlier Labour Government Bill had provided for the precise opposite). This leaves the enforceability of collective agreements made before December 1971 and oral agreements to be settled by the previous law.

The definition of a collective agreement is wide. It includes (s. 166) "any agreement or arrangement" made "in whatever way and whatever form" by or on behalf of trade unions and employers or employers' associations which either prescribes terms and conditions of employment or is a procedure agreement within the definition in the Act. Section 35 contains provisions dealing with the resolutions of Joint Industrial Councils and similar bodies. It is a fair assumption that the consequence of any sort of industrial relations activity will be within s. 34 if reduced to writing. But there is no difficulty about avoiding legal liability: any clause, however expressed, even if it only relates to some of the agreement, will be effective in that regard. But documents may be caught by s. 34 that are not thought of as collective agreements at all—minutes of a meeting of stewards with management, for example.

"Legally enforceable" does not mean enforceable by ordinary action in the ordinary courts. Section 129 specifically states that only NIRC may take jurisdiction over collective agreements, and under s. 36 breach of a legally enforceable collective agreement (oral or in writing, whether or not made after the Act) is declared to be an unfair industrial practice. This means that, under s. 101, any person "against whom the action was taken" may take proceedings in NIRC for a declaration, compensation or a "desist order".

As we said earlier, the enforceability of collective agreements is really a question relating to procedure agreements, and procedures are more often broken by the workers for whom the agreements were made than by the unions who made them. So s. 36 goes further and makes the parties to the agreement to some extent insurers of it. It is also an unfair indus-

trial practice for a party not to take all such steps as are
reasonably practicable to:

> (*a*) prevent its members, or persons acting on its behalf,
> or purporting to do so, from acting "contrary to an
> undertaking given by that party";
> (*b*) where such action has occurred, stop it and prevent
> its recurrence.

Presumably, the "undertaking" has to relate specifically to the
action taken. But a "no-strike" undertaking given by a union
covers unofficial action too (s. 36(3)).

Although legally enforceable collective agreements are not
unknown, it would appear that, since the Act, the clause
excluding all legal liability has become the norm.

II   PROCEDURE AGREEMENTS

The Act clearly assumes a public interest in procedure
agreements. By s. 58 the Minister is empowered to make regulations (which have not yet been made) requiring employers
to report their procedure agreements to the Ministry. Section
58 imposes a criminal sanction in respect of such a duty. This,
in fact, will very probably operate to give statutory force to
existing voluntary arrangements among larger companies.

In the circumstances, it would be strange if the task of promoting efficient procedures were left entirely to the parties.
It is not. The Act contains provisions for "remedial action"
in respect of bad procedures. But first it is necessary to consider the Act's definition of procedure agreement, which is
wide.

The definition is in s. 166(5). A procedure agreement
is those parts of a collective agreement (whose definition is
described above) which relate to any of the following:

> (*a*) Consultation, arbitration or negotiation machinery for
> terms and conditions of employment (i.e. "claims"
> procedures).

(*b*) Consultation, arbitration or negotiation machinery for other questions arising between employers and workers or unions.

(*c*) Negotiating rights. (This term is discussed later.)

(*d*) Facilities for union officials (including shop stewards).

(*e*) Dismissal procedures.

(*f*) Other disciplinary procedures.

(*g*) Individual grievance procedures.

Very little comment is needed, save to point out the breadth of the coverage of the definition.

The remedial action may be taken by the Minister, the employer or any registered trade union which has negotiating rights or is a party to a procedure agreement (s. 37(2)). An unregistered union may not initiate the action. The Minister must consult with the employer and any appropriate registered union if it is he who takes action, and conversely any other person or body must give notice to the Minister before making application, and the Minister may "advise and assist". Action is taken by way of application to NIRC. Applications may be made on one of three grounds:

(i) There is no procedure agreement.

(ii) The procedure agreement that does exist is unsuitable for settling disputes or grievances "promptly and fairly".

(iii) A procedure agreement exists but is broken by industrial action.

Applications are made in respect of a "unit of employment", which is defined in a roundabout way as a business or part of a business (see s. 37(6) and s. 167). This is less than a whole industry but may be more than the employees of a single employer.

If NIRC is satisfied either that industrial relations have been "seriously impeded" or that there have been "substantial and repeated losses of working time" because of the defects alleged, then the matter is referred to the CIR. The CIR's task is to discover whether the defects alleged are in fact correct and, if so, to suggest a remedy. It has wide powers. The scope of its terms of reference may be extended if necessary (s. 38). Its aim is to promote discussions between "parties to the reference". "Parties to the reference" are parties to any existing procedure agreement together with other employers or registered employers' associations or registered unions as are thought appropriate by the CIR (s. 39). The CIR is directed to try to get the parties to agree to provisions "capable of having effect as a legally enforceable contract" (s. 39(3)), but whether or not it achieves that desired result, if it is satisfied that a solution to the problem has been reached, it may report back to NIRC and the reference is withdrawn (s. 39(4)). Otherwise, the CIR proceeds to draw up its own solution, incorporating whatever may have been agreed. This, in the form of a legally enforceable collective agreement, is referred back to NIRC (s. 40). This "agreement" can be put into effect by order of NIRC, but such an order can only be made if an application is made by an employer or by a registered trade union party to the "agreement" within six months of the report (s. 41).

The procedure is cumbrous and, judged in terms of its end results, probably unlikely to be very efficient. Its importance, however, is more likely to lie in the fact that the Minister is hereby given very substantial powers of investigation into procedures where industrial relations seem not to be good.

III   NEGOTIATING

So far we have been considering the formal structures within which collective bargaining takes place. We must now turn to the process itself. There is not a very great deal that the law can do with regard to this, however. In the end, the matter is one for voluntary agreement. The U.S. National Labor Relations Act of 1935 (the Wagner Act) imposed a general obligation on employers to engage in bona fide collective bargaining with appropriate unions. The Industrial Relations Act does not go so far. It provides for one small example of compulsory recognition, the Sole Bargaining

Agency, but it makes assumptions that voluntary systems will operate around this.

Like much else in the Act, these provisions are concerned with a unit of workers, here called a "bargaining unit". This and other notions are defined in s. 44. A bargaining unit is first defined as a group of employees of the same employer, or of legally related employers in a "multi-company" (so-called "associated employers"; see s. 267(8)), such as can appropriately be bargained about as a unit. What makes a unit "appropriate" is tentatively defined in the Code of Practice, paras. 74–81, which suggest ten factors to be taken into account. They are:

1 The nature of the work.
2 Training, experience and qualifications of the workers.
3 Common interests.
4 The wishes of the workers concerned.
5 Organisation and place of work.
6 Hours, working arrangements and payment systems.
7 The matters to be bargained about.
8 Union and management organisation.
9 Existing bargaining arrangements.
10 The problem of supervisory workers who may represent management.

This permits a very great variety of different types of bargaining unit. All that is required is that it should be defined according to some functional principle.

The bargaining unit is essentially the workplace. The bargaining there takes place subject to "more extensive bargaining arrangements", which phrase refers, in effect, to national agreements. The workers in the unit must all work for the same employer (or an associated employer).

The Act envisages several possible levels of recognition within the bargaining unit. The employer may confer "negotiating rights" on a union or panel of unions. The Act has little to say about negotiating rights. It defines them as the "right to participate, on behalf of all or some of the employees comprised in the bargaining unit, in negotiations relating to that unit, with a view to the conclusion or modification of one or more collective agreements". It is a right to negotiate, not merely to be consulted. The Act does not specifically say how negotiating rights may be granted. Presumably unless they are granted as part of a legally enforceable collective agreement, the withdrawal of negotiating rights by an employer will not have any legal consequences. Nor does the possession of negotiating rights receive detailed treatment: it is, however, a condition precedent for applications for a compulsory Agency Shop (s. 11(3)), for initiating remedial action on procedure agreements (s. 37(2)) and for receiving the benefit for a lawful recommendation from an employer that his employees join a union (s. 5(3)).

The level above the grant of "negotiating rights" is the voluntary recognition of a "Sole Bargaining Agent". This is nothing more complicated than the grant of *exclusive* negotiating rights to a union, registered or unregistered, or a joint panel of unions, within a unit. Again, this is not dealt with in explicit detail in the Act, merely assumed. As with the grant of simple negotiating rights, there is no formal requirement for the creation of a voluntary Sole Bargaining Agency, but unless it is done by legally enforceable collective agreement, no legal consequences will ensue if recognition is withdrawn.

Finally, comes the compulsory Sole Bargaining Agency. This can come into existence as a result of a procedure similar in kind to that used for improving procedure agreements. It involves the CIR, it is cumbrous and long drawn-out and at every stage encourages the parties to settle their differences by agreement. The procedure is initiated by an application to NIRC under s. 45. Such an application may be made by a registered union (or unions), by an employer, jointly by a registered union and an employer, or by the Minister. The Minister may not apply without first consulting the employer and the union or unions (registered or unregistered) concerned. If others apply, the Minister must have notice and be given the opportunity to "advise and assist". The application is that two questions be referred to the CIR: whether a unit should be recognised as a bargaining unit and whether any union or panel of unions (registered or unregistered) should be recognised as sole bargaining agent for the unit. The questions are only referred to the CIR if NIRC is satisfied that the employers and unions have tried to settle the questions themselves first (s. 46).

The CIR (whose terms of reference may be amended: s. 47) then investigates and reports back to NIRC, with copies to the Minister, the employer and all relevant trade unions (s. 48(2)). The CIR may not recommend as a Sole Bargaining Agent a union which is not independent or which does not enjoy the support of the majority of those in the unit (s. 48(4). But it has very wide powers and may recommend as sole bargaining agent any union, registered or unregistered, or a panel of unions, registered, unregistered or mixed, so long as the agent has the support and the resources necessary. It may impose conditions.

Once the report is with NIRC, there are six months in which an application might be made to put it into effect. Here, for the first time in this connection, unregistered trade unions are firmly discriminated against. No application may be made unless, at the time of the application, the union named as a Sole Bargaining Agent is registered. If a joint panel is recommended, every union that is a member of that panel must be registered at the time of the application (s. 49(2)). Subject to this, either employer or union may apply (s. 48 (1)).

If an application is made, the matter is referred back to the CIR, which supervises a ballot in the unit. If a majority of those voting is in favour of the report, NIRC makes an order putting it into effect (s. 50). When an order is in force, it is an unfair industrial practice for an employer to bargain with any other union in respect of that unit or for the employer "not to take all such action, by way of or with a view to carrying on collective bargaining with" the named trade union "as might reasonably be expected to be taken by an employer ready and willing to carry on such collective bargaining" (s. 55(1)). It is also an unfair industrial practice to take or threaten industrial action with a view to compelling the employer to commit those unfair industrial practices (s. 55(3)). Thus, under s. 101, any person (including a union) against whom such action was taken may apply to NIRC for a declaration, compensation or a "desist order".

Even if no application (and therefore no order) is made, the CIR's report is not totally without effect. For two years after the report, it is an unfair industrial practice for any person, including unions and officials, to take or threaten industrial action to compel an employer to recognise or bargain with any union other than that union or unions (registered or unregistered) which were recommended in the report (s. 55(6))—which gives a recommended unregistered union some protection.

All this relates to starting new Sole Bargaining Agencies or confirming existing ones. The Act also contains provisions for questioning the value of existing systems. Any employee within a unit may apply to NIRC on the grounds that a union or unions (registered or unregistered) recognised by the employer as a Sole Bargaining Agent does not adequately represent the employees in the unit (s. 51). These applications must be supported by the written concurrence of one-fifth of the unit where the Sole Bargaining Agency is voluntary, and two-fifths if an order has been made: in the latter case, no application at all can be made within two years of the order. The CIR investigates and seeks to promote a voluntary settlement (s. 52(2)). If it fails, it then considers whether the unit should be split for the purpose of a ballot on the application, or whether a single ballot should be held. If a single ballot is held, it is held on the question whether the existing Sole Bargaining Agency should continue, and if a majority voting vote against the Sole Bargaining Agent, an order is made prohibiting recognition for two years (s. 52; s. 53(1)). If a split ballot is held and a section votes against the Agent, an order is made in respect of that section (s. 52; s. 53(2)).

The CIR in investigating applications to change existing systems has really to be convinced that the representation is not adequate, which will generally require detailed evidence and will constitute a complicated factual issue. Nor does this type of application necessarily advance the claims of any other body, since the result is the destruction of the existing arrangements and not the creation of new ones. Indeed, s. 53(5) prohibits further applications to set up new agencies, under s. 45, for two years after an order is made under s. 53.

IV INFORMATION

The ready disclosure of information is generally regarded as providing a firm basis for good industrial relations. The Industrial Relations Act contains two sections which impose upon employers the duty to give information. At the time of writing, neither section has been brought into effect.

Section 56 will require that, when collective bargaining is in progress, every employer disclose to the authorised representatives of any registered union with whom he is bargaining all information relating to his business that is in his possession (or the possession of an "associated employer") which it would be good industrial relations practice to disclose and without which the union representative would be "to a material extent impeded" in his bargaining. Failure can lead to a complaint to NIRC. NIRC may make a declaration, issue a mandatory order to the employer, or allow the union claim, about which the bargaining was going on, to be presented unilaterally by the union to the IAB for arbitration.

Section 56 is not precise as to what information should be disclosed. It will be supplemented by the Code of Practice. The present Code states simply that management should comply with all reasonable requests for information. It also states that the section will be put into effect when the report of the CIR on the question of disclosure of information has been received and proper consultation with interested bodies held.

Section 57 will impose upon businesses employing more than 350 persons the duty to make an annual written report to all employees containing information to be specified in regulations to be made by the Minister. The Code of Practice, however, already recommends (see paras. 54–64) that employees should be kept informed not only of matters directly affecting their jobs, such as discipline, promotions, trade union arrangements, etc., but also the performance and plans of the establishment where they work and the business for which they work. This is, of course, not a full-scale legal obligation.

Oddly, although the duties to disclose information have not

yet been put into effect, the limitations to those duties have. Section 158 enacts that no employer shall "by virtue of s. 56 or s. 57" be required to disclose:

(*a*) matters affecting national security;

(*b*) matters which it would be illegal to disclose;

(*c*) information communicated to the employer in confidence;

(*d*) information relating specifically to an individual, unless that individual consents;

(*e*) information "seriously prejudicial" to the employer's business, except in respect of collective bargaining; or

(*f*) information obtained in connection with legal proceedings.

At present the immunities undoubtedly exceed the obligation.

Chapter 8

The Legal Consequences of Industrial Action

I INTRODUCTION

Except in times of emergency, industrial action has virtually no consequences in public law. The special crimes developed in the last century of which strikers were almost always guilty have either been abolished or have fallen into complete disuse. In his evidence to the Donovan Commission, Sir Harold Emmerson, former Permanent Secretary to the Ministry of Labour, gave an amusing account of the fiasco that occurred when the Government decided to prosecute some Kent miners for striking illegally under wartime legislation in 1942. The evidence was printed as an appendix to the report, presumably as an awful warning.

But this was not always so. In the last century, every strike was a crime and almost all peripheral activity engaged in by participants in industrial action could be said to amount to one or other of the vague common law offences of "obstruction", "molestation" or "intimidation". The legal history of industrial relations has, to a very large extent, been a history of the removal of such sanctions. The process was continued by the Industrial Relations Act 1971, which removed one of the last vestiges of criminal strikes—the provision in the Conspiracy and Protection of Property Act 1875 which made strikes in the "public utilities" (gas, water and, later, electricity) normally criminal. The companion subsection, (s. 3(2)) remains, although it is in practice a dead letter. It provides that it shall be an offence for a person "wilfully and maliciously" to break his contract of employment if he knows or has reasonable cause to believe that the probable consequences will be to endanger life or limb, or to expose valuable property to destruction or serious damage. The 1875 Act also preserved five rather archaic crimes relating to the conduct of industrial action, but rounded them off with the qualification that the right of peaceful picketing was to be guaranteed.

This guarantee now appears in s. 134 of the Industrial Relations Act. This enacts that where one or more persons "in contemplation or furtherance of an industrial dispute" (see p. 114 for an explanation of this term) attend at or near a place of work or "any other place where a person happens to be, not being a place where he resides" only for the purpose of peacefully communicating or obtaining information or peacefully persuading a person to work or not to work, that shall not be a crime either under the Conspiracy and Protection of Property Act, nor any other enactment or rule of the law. It is not, of course, an absolute immunity. A picket who commits murder is still a murderer, if only because, while murdering, he is not "peacefully persuading" within the meaning of s. 134. But lines are hard to draw.

> Mr. Broome was a trade union official. He organised a picket at a building site during a building workers' strike. He attempted to persuade a driver not to deliver to the site. The driver drove off and manoeuvred his lorry to enter the site. Mr. Broome stood in front of the lorry. He was charged with obstructing the highway and the Divisional Court held him guilty. His only right was to attempt to persuade with words, not to obstruct, however peacefully.
>
> *Hunt* v. *Broome* (1973) DC

If the criminal law of industrial action is dead, the civil law is not. The primary legal question in relation to civil proceedings is whether the industrial action in question was or was not a breach of the contract of employment of the employer or workers taking part in it. It is this question which lies at the root of the practical legal problems in this field, although in its own terms it is almost as academic as the question of the criminality of strikes.

It is not possible to give an accurate general answer. It depends on the contract and the industrial action in question. Prima facie it would seem that most strikes would be breaches of contract: they amount to a repudiation of what must be regarded as the central obligation of the worker—the obligation to work when called upon to do so. But even here all is not entirely clear. There may be a term in the contract permitting the strike. It is, of course, highly unlikely that such a term would be expressly agreed, but it could possibly be implied—from long, albeit reluctantly, accepted practice, or from the incorporation of an elaborate disputes procedure which, by outlawing strike action until the procedure has been used, could be said implicitly to permit it after. Then there is the question of strike notice. For some time judicial opinion was divided upon strike notice. One view held that it could be treated as equivalent to notice of termination, whereby the strikers, as it were, terminated their contracts temporarily. The other view pointed to the differences between going on strike and leaving one's job (see *Stratford* v. *Lindley* (1964) CA; *Morgan* v. *Fry* (1968) CA). The Industrial Relations Act has settled the dispute by statutorily granting the right to give strike notice (s. 147). The notice must be at least of the length necessary to terminate the contract of employment in question (*i.e.,* where the Contracts of Employment Act 1963 applies, at least one week) and, if given, the strike will not be treated as a breach of contract nor will the strike notice be treated as notice to terminate the contract completely. It is nothing but effective strike notice. All this is subject to the contract. Section 147 will not apply to strikes prohibited by a term of the contract, express or implied, which clearly covers strikes which are "unconstitutional" under a procedure agreement effectively incorporated into the contracts of employment of the strikers.

Other forms of industrial action are more difficult. Lockouts are the legal converse of a strike. If the one is a breach of contract, so must be the other. But there is no provision equivalent to s. 147 which gives the employer the right to give "lock-out notice". Further, it is clear that, as a matter of strict law, the right to suspend must be conferred by a term of the contract, or a suspension, for whatever reason, will constitute a breach of contract (*Hanley* v. *Pease and Partners* (1915) KB).

Lesser forms of industrial action cause more difficulty. It is perhaps easy to see how deliberate obstruction of the employers' interests, by slowing down production, could be a breach of contract. But other types of action cause their own problems:

> In pursuit of an industrial dispute, the railway unions banned overtime, refused rest-day and Sunday work, worked strictly to the British Railways rule-book and did nothing but normal duties. This action was held to involve breaches of contract, not only because the workers overstepped their strict rights in several minor respects, but also because there was an implied term in their contracts of employment that they would interpret and apply the strict terms (*e.g.* the rule-book) in a reasonable way and not obstructively.

Secretary of State v. *ASLEF (No. 2)* 1972 CA

> Mr. Morgan left the TGWU and joined a small dockworkers breakaway body. The officials of the union instructed their members to continue their work insofar as they could without working with Mr. Morgan and others in his position. Due to the drawn-out negotiations, the employers had several weeks' notice of this action and were not entirely out of sympathy with the Union's point of view. Of the three members of the Court of Appeal, one said there was a breach of the contracts of employment of the members who obeyed the instruction, one said there was not because a change in those terms had been successfully negotiated by implication, and one said that the "strike notice" prevented the action being a breach of contract.

Morgan v. *Fry* (1968) CA

What finally makes the question whether industrial action is a breach of contract academic is a decision by the Court of Appeal in 1958 (*NCB* v. *Galley*). With the possible exception of certain kinds of production workers whose product can easily be identified, the damages an employer will receive in respect of the breach of contract committed by a striker is the individual cost of his replacement for the days in question. No account is to be taken of any facts other than the absence of that single individual from work. This makes the suing of strikers (each individually) a highly unprofitable exercise.

II TORTS

If an employer, or other person injured by industrial action, wishes to sue for damages, the law of contract at best offers him only a series of useless actions against individual strikers. The law of tort, on the other hand, may give him an action against a strike leader for having brought about the industrial action and so caused the damage. The field is a relatively new one and the torts are still developing, but four clear heads of liability have been established, together with several possible future developments.

Conspiracy

This is the oldest idea in the list, although it first appeared in the criminal law. The principle is twofold. First, if A, B and C agree together to carry out some unlawful act to the damage of X, then X should be able to sue all three, whosoever actually executed the plan. To put it into lay language, they were all in it together. And if we are to ask what C, who only agreed to the plan but did nothing further, did that was wrongful or tortious, the answer must be that he conspired, and that is the wrong. The second aspect leads on from here. If it is the conspiracy that is wrongful, why should X not be able to sue if, by some chance, the means used by the conspirators to injure him were not themselves quite unlawful? This proposition was accepted by the House of Lords in *Quinn* v. *Leathem* in 1901, where a meat trade workers' union, in pursuit of a dispute with a wholesale meat purveyor, effectively persuaded a retailer not to put in his usual order. This was "simple" conspiracy, and the officials were liable.

To this general principle one important qualification was added: there was no liability where the defendants were simply acting in pursuance of their own legitimate interests and not maliciously harassing the plaintiff. This was clearly applied to trade unions in *Crofter Hand Woven Harris Tweed* v. *Veitch* in 1942 by the House of Lords, who held that the action of union officials in blacking the supplies of a competitor of their employer in order to secure a new pay agreement and a closed shop from him was not actionable. They had acted to protect their own interests as unionists rather than to damage the competitor.

The potential application of this general tort to industrial action is substantial, but because of the effect of the statutory immunities which have existed since 1906 (see p. 113), its practical usefulness has been small.

Direct Inducement of Breach of Contract

In 1853 a court gave an action to the proprietor of one theatre against the proprietor of another who had induced a singer to break her contract with the first and sing for him (*Lumley* v. *Gye* (1853) QB). He had directly induced her to break her contract. The application of this to a strike or any other industrial action that involves a breach of the contract of employment is clear. But again, because of the statutory immunities, it has little practical importance. It seems likely that, as in conspiracy, the courts might recognise cases in which such inducement might be justified, although the occasions seem rare and possibly limited to circumstances of genuine moral justification (see *Scala Ballroom* v. *Ratcliffe* (1958) QB (action against colour bar); *Brimelow* v. *Casson* (1924) ChD (action against employer whose low rates of pay drove his employees to destitution and degradation)).

Indirect Inducement of a Breach of Contract

Because the original statutory immunity only applied to the

inducement of breaches of a contract of employment, it proved possible to develop a second species of the tort in cases where industrial action was taken *indirectly* by, for instance, blacking an employer and thus causing the breach of supply contracts entered into by other employers. This would not be covered. But the union officials would be very unlikely *directly* to induce suppliers to break their contracts. They are more likely to "warn" or "inform" them and do it indirectly. The extension was accepted as good by the Court of Appeal in 1952 (*Thompson (D. C.) and Co. Ltd.* v. *Deakin* (1952) CA): a case where the defendants "warned" Messrs. Bowater that, since there was a dispute with the newspaper publishers D. C. Thompson, their drivers who were u..ion members might not be willing to deliver newsprint to Thompsons. Bowaters broke their contract. Thompsons sued, but were unsuccessful.

The reason why the action failed was that the Court required further elements for liability. Mere indirect inducement was not to be actionable unless unlawful means were used. The most obvious candidate for unlawful means in the context is the breach of contract that would very likely occur if a strike were actually called. More recent cases have shown that the courts may be satisfied by more attenuated forms of illegality: holding to a restrictive trading agreement likely to be declared void under the Restrictive Trade Practices Act in *Daily Mirror* v. *Gardner* (1968) CA for example. (However, the mere fact that the action constitutes an unfair industrial practice under the Industrial Relations Act was apparently held not sufficient "unlawfulness" for an analogous tort in *Cory Lighterage* v. *TGWU* (1973) CA.)

The main problem with indirect inducement is that, by definition, the defendant is not directly concerned with the contract whose breach is being induced. To begin with the courts seem to have required that, before the defendant was liable, he must intend the breach he caused. Which implies some knowledge. However, in *Emerald Construction* v. *Lowthian* (1966) CA, the Court of Appeal allowed an action to succeed against a defendant who had intended the contract to come to an end, preferably without breach, but without caring greatly one way or the other.

This inevitably led on to another point. If the defendant is to be liable because he acted so as to interfere with a contract, even when he did not know the terms of the contract and did not intend it to be broken, there seems no reason *not* to hold him liable if, by chance, the contract was not really broken at all. This happened in *Torquay Hotels* v. *Cousins* (1969) CA, where oil supply contracts to a hotel were interfered with. No breaches were caused, partly because no order was given which was not in fact performed and partly because the contract contained an effective industrial disputes clause relieving the oil company of liability in the case of an industrial dispute. But the union officials were still held liable.

So indirect inducement of a breach of contract might better be described as indirectly interfering with contractual relations, whether or not breaches are caused, by wrongful means.

Intimidation

Intimidation was an old tort resuscitated in 1964 by the House of Lords in *Rookes* v. *Barnard*. There the defendants had told BOAC that unless one of their draughtsmen, the plaintiff, was dismissed, there would be an immediate strike (which would undoubtedly have involved breaches of contracts of employment) among the other draughtsmen. Mr. Rookes was given proper notice. No contract had been broken, no unlawful means actually used. But the defendants were held liable for the *threat* of unlawful action. Thus the tort is constituted if A unlawfully threatens B so as to induce B to injure C. It has also been suggested (see *Stratford* v. *Lindley* (1964) CA (1965) HL) that if B stands firm and suffers loss himself rather than injure C, he should be able to sue A for *direct* intimidation, but the law does not yet seem to have reached that position.

Other Development

In the great case of *Allen* v. *Flood* in 1898, the whole House of Lords, having heard the opinions of all the Queen's Bench judges, decided by a majority, that, in the absence of conspiracy, induced breach of contract, or other unlawfulness, a trade unionist was not to be liable simply because his action had injured someone. There was to be no simple tort of injuring someone's business or employment or trade. This decision was not universally accepted by the judges and, in one sense, the gradual liberalisation of the torts discussed above shows a movement against the *Allen* v. *Flood* policy. In recent cases there have been several suggestions that it might be actionable to interfere with a man's trade directly, or indirectly, if unlawful means were used. The fact that the Industrial Relations Act contains alternative methods of proceeding against strikers may well reduce the possibilities of these developments, but it may not.

III IMMUNITIES

Since 1906 the law has granted immunities from civil proceedings in industrial disputes. They were of two kinds. The first is now to be found in the Industrial Relations Act, ss. 132 and 167. Section 132 enacts that "an act done by a person in contemplation or furtherance of an industrial dispute" shall not be actionable in four situations.

(i) It will not constitute direct or indirect inducement of a breach of contract (employment or otherwise) or "interference" with such a contract.

(ii) It will not constitute the tort of intimidation, insofar as the threat is a threat that a contract (employment or otherwise) will be broken or interfered with.

(iii) "For the avoidance of doubt" it is declared that such an act will not be actionable as "an interference with the trade, business or employment of another person or with the right of another person to dispose of his capital or his labour as he wills". This provision dates from 1906. It has never been applied and often avoided.

(iv) It will not constitute a "simple" conspiracy. The act which the conspirators conspire to do must itself be actionable in tort.

This is not complete. There are gaps and uncertainties, and with the law in a state of flux such gaps and uncertainties are not likely to decrease. The defences are available to trade unions, registered or not, or to individuals. But they are only available when the act was done "in contemplation or furtherance of an industrial dispute". "Industrial dispute" is defined in s. 167 as a dispute between employers (or their associations) and unions (registered or not) or individual workers, which relates "wholly or mainly" to:

(*a*) terms and conditions of employment or physical conditions of work;

(*b*) engagement, non-engagement, termination or suspension of individual workers;

(*c*) allocation of work between workers; or

(*d*) a procedure agreement, as defined in the Act.

The definition of a procedure agreement has already been discussed (see p. 96): most of the rest is fairly clear. However:

> Mr. Shute, a lighterman, where there is a long tradition of a closed shop, left the union because he disapproved of the system. His employers suspended him on full pay. It was said in the course of the judgements in the Court of Appeal that there could be no industrial dispute in the case. "Terms and conditions" referred to contractual terms upon which a man might be required to work: there was no dispute about such terms in Mr. Shute's case. "Suspension" means suspension from both work and pay and is similarly irrelevant.
>
> *Cory Lighterage* v. *TGWU* (1973) CA

The second immunity was enjoyed by trade unions from 1906 to 1971. Union funds were generally protected from claims for damages in tort, whether or not there was an industrial dispute. This has been abolished by the Industrial Relations Act. The Act does, however, make it clear that, registered or not, individual trade unionists are not to be personally liable for damages awarded against the union, nor will any provident fund that cannot be used for financing industrial action.

IV   UNFAIR INDUSTRIAL PRACTICES

As a matter of policy, the Industrial Relations Act describes all actions which are contrary to its provisions to be "unfair industrial practices". The term is applied even to unfair dismissals. Many of these 27 or so unfair industrial practices may involve industrial action, however. They can be divided into five groups.

(*a*) Breach of a legally enforceable collective agreement under s. 36(1), failure to take reasonable steps to prevent others from acting contrary to an undertaking in it (s. 36(2)), etc. These do not necessarily involve industrial action, but almost always will. The details have been discussed earlier at p. 94.

(*b*) Various acts in sabotage of the institutions and procedures of the Act (*e.g.* organising industrial action to induce an employer not to apply for an agency shop ballot under s. 16(2) (*b*)). There are some 13 of these, all involving industrial action. See ss. 13(2), 16(1), (2) (*a*) and (*b*), 33(3) (*a*), (*b*), (*c*) and (*d*), 55(3), (4) (*b*), (6), (7) and (8). Several of these have been mentioned at appropriate points in the book. They are of little general interest.

(c) Under s. 96 it is an unfair industrial practice, in contemplation or furtherance of an industrial dispute, knowingly to induce another person to break a contract unless the inducer is a registered trade union or an official authorised under the rules of a registered trade union acting within his authority. The contract may be a contract of employment, a supply contract (for the "induced person" may be a company) but not a collective agreement. The aim here is to discourage unofficial action, but the unfair industrial practice also covers official action taken by unregistered unions.

(*d*) Under s. 97 it is an unfair industrial practice for any person, including a union, registered or unregistered, to organise or threaten industrial action in support of another unfair industrial practice, unless the "defendant" is a registered trade union and the act supported is an unfair industrial practice only by virtue of s. 96. Section 97 applies only to acts in contemplation or furtherance of an industrial dispute.

(*e*) Under s. 98 it is an unfair industrial practice to take "blacking" action in contemplation or furtherance of an industrial dispute. "Blacking" is closely and rather confusingly defined as taking industrial action to induce X to break a contract of his, or to prevent him from performing it, when X is an "extraneous party" to the dispute. An "extraneous party" to a dispute is a person, not a party to it, who has not taken any "action in material support" of a party. "Action in material support" is not defined, but the Act does declare that it is *not*: being an associated employer in a "multi-company"; being a member of the same employers' association as a party; having contributed to a support fund without specific reference to the dispute; not having supplied goods or services under a contract entered into beforehand.

Categories (*b*), (*d*) and (*e*) all involve organising or threatening industrial action. This is defined by the Act as follows:

(i) calling, organising, procuring or financing a strike;
(ii) organising, procuring or financing any irregular industrial action short of a strike;
(iii) instituting, carrying on, organising, procuring or financing a lock-out.

Or, in every case, threatening such action. The definition is extremely wide.

"Strike" is defined in s. 167 as a "concerted stoppage of work" in contemplation or furtherance of an industrial dispute, whether or not a breach of contract, or even termination of employment, is involved. "Lock-out" has a similar non-contractual definition as action in contemplation or furtherance of an industrial dispute by one or more employers by way of any sort of exclusion, suspension or termination of the employment of a group of workers. "Irregular industrial action short of a strike" is defined in s. 33(4) as concerted action by workers (other than a strike) in contemplation or furtherance of an industrial dispute, aimed at preventing, reducing or interfering with production, carried on in breach of the contracts of employment of some or all of them. Thus it relates back to the question raised at the beginning of this chapter (see p. 106). The ASLEF case, there mentioned, shows how a "work to rule" may yet constitute a piece of "irregular industrial action short of a strike".

Most unfair industrial practices (except breach, etc., of a legally enforceable collective agreement) are only constituted by action taken in contemplation or furtherance of an industrial dispute (either by the express provisions of the appropriate section or indirectly through the definitions of "strike", etc.). This makes a distinction of jurisdiction. Unfair industrial practices are a matter for NIRC under s. 101 of the Act: they will generally occur when there is an industrial dispute, within the meaning of s. 167: which means that the defences under s. 132 apply and no action will be possible in the ordinary courts. There are possible overlaps, however. An unfair industrial practice might occasionally occur with no industrial dispute: a tort might be committed which is still actionable during an industrial dispute because it does not come precisely within the terms of s. 132. Accordingly the Act in s. 131 confers on the ordinary courts a power to stay tort proceedings before them if either proceedings have already been brought in NIRC or an industrial tribunal on the matter, or proceedings could be brought as the matter constitutes an unfair industrial practice. In *Midland Cold Storage* v. *Steer* (1972) ChD, Megarry, J., made it quite clear that he thought that the discretion ought to be exercised in favour of staying the proceedings in the ordinary courts, unless there was good reason to act otherwise.

Additionally, in any case of tortious conspiracy, the ordinary court *must* stay proceedings either if proceedings in NIRC or a tribunal have begun, or the facts constitute an unfair industrial practice.

V   PROCEEDINGS IN NIRC

In respect of any unfair industrial practice any person against whom the action was taken may make a complaint to NIRC under s. 101. NIRC has three remedies to hand and a wide discretion. It may issue a declaration of the rights of the parties, award compensation or make a "desist" order, directing the respondent to refrain from the action in question.

Registered trade unions enjoy certain privileges at this point. NIRC may not award compensation or issue a "desist" order against an official of a registered union acting within the scope of his authority. "Official" includes shop steward. Officials of unregistered unions are not protected. Further, registered unions have a form of limited liability in respect of awards of compensation by NIRC. There is a sliding scale:

With less than 5,000 members	£5,000
5,000, but less than 25,000	£25,000
25,000, but less than 100,000	£50,000
100,000 or more	£100,000

In practice, the sanction which has been used most dramatically by NIRC has been the power to punish (by fine and imprisonment) for contempt of its orders. This is not specifically provided for in the Act, but arises from the fact that NIRC is a part of the High Court.

VI EMERGENCIES

In time of war, and in emergency in peacetime, governments commonly take wide powers to control the normal processes of bargaining and disputes. In England, the peacetime emergency powers are found primarily in the Emergency Powers Acts 1920 and 1964. Under these Acts, the Government is empowered to declare a state of emergency if events have occurred "calculated . . . to deprive the community of the essential of life". In practice states of emergency are declared in time of very serious industrial action.

During a state of emergency (which may last only for one month, but is renewable) Parliament must be called, and the Government may govern by Order in Council laid before Parliament. There are only three limitations upon what may be done:

(i) there must be no fining or imprisonment without trial;

(ii) there must be no military or industrial conscription; and

(iii) striking or peaceful picketing must not be made criminal.

In addition, the Government may choose to deal with a state of emergency by using the armed forces. This power is now contained in the Emergency Powers Act 1964. Of course, no regulations may be made, no penalties imposed, but work can be carried out by the soldiers.

The Industrial Relations Act, in a part (Part VIII) owing much to the U.S. Taft-Hartley Act, provides the Government with further emergency procedures. These are far more complicated. The Secretary of State for Employment may apply to NIRC for one or both of two orders: a "cooling-off" order or a "strike ballot" order. He may apply for a cooling-off order if industrial action in contemplation or furtherance of an industrial dispute has begun or is likely to begin which appears to him to be so disruptive as to be likely to:

(*a*) be gravely injurious to the national economy; or

(*b*) to imperil national security; or

(*c*) to create a serious risk of public disorder; or

(*d*) to endanger life or health.

NIRC must grant the order if there are sufficient grounds for believing that the Minister is right in his belief. The wording of the Act gives little discretion, and this was confirmed on the only occasion (at the time of writing) when these powers were used. In that case (*Secretary of State* v. *ASLEF* (1972) CA) it was held that a court could only disagree with the Minister if it was satisfied that, in the circumstances, no reasonable Minister could have come to that conclusion, which is tantamount to saying that NIRC has no discretion at all.

NIRC does have some discretion in specifying the terms of the order, however. The order must specify the "area of employment" within which it is to apply, name the names of those to be bound by it, and set its time limit, not exceeding 60 days. Only leaders may be named. While the order remains in force no person named may organise industrial action or threaten to do so. That constitutes contempt of court.

A ballot order is obtained by a similar procedure. However, while a cooling-off order may technically be applied for in a lock-out, a ballot order only issues for a strike or irregular industrial action short of a strike. Further, the Minister must also be satisfied that "there are reasons for doubting whether the workers taking part . . . are taking parting in it in accordance with their wishes". Finally, a ballot may be ordered not only when the action may be injurious to the national economy, etc., but also if it may seriously injure the livelihood of a substantial number of workers. As mentioned in connection with cooling-off orders, however, it would be extremely difficult to challenge the Minister's opinion in NIRC or any other court. NIRC orders the ballot and specifies the area of employment, the question to be asked and the time allowed for the operation. During that time no trade union or employer may take or threaten industrial action among the workers who are to vote. The ballot is conducted by a recognised registered union that is appropriate by virtue of its membership, or by any other body (including an unregistered union) under the supervision of the union, or by the Commission. Naturally, it might be expected that the appropriate union or unions will conduct the ballot: this occurred in the Railway case.

There are no teeth to the ballot. The results are simply declared.

Chapter 9

Employers' Liability

I THE MEANING OF "EMPLOYERS' LIABILITY"

Employers' liability is imposed on an employer by law because of his status as an employer. It is not a technical legal term but is a useful portmanteau expression. It includes liability for certain acts of negligence on the employer's part and by some classes of employee for whom the law holds him responsible whilst they are carrying out their duties. It also covers special liabilities imposed by statute.

To understand employers' liability it is, therefore, necessary to understand the law of negligence and the concept of breach of statutory duty.

II NEGLIGENCE

Negligence is a tort: an obligation imposed by law (as opposed to one voluntarily entered into such as a contract) which gives rise to an action for damages if the obligation is not fulfilled and damage results. It is a difficult concept to define or even to explain. The classical definition dates back to 1856:

> "The omission to do something which a reasonable man, guided upon those considerations which ordinarily regulate the conduct of human affairs, would do, or doing something which a reasonable and prudent man would not do"

> (Alderson, B., in *Blyth* v. *Birmingham Waterworks Company* (1856) Ex Ch).

This dictum illustrates the problems of the tort. It is clear enough what it is all about: "reasonable" behaviour. It is also obvious that the specification of what constitutes "reasonable" behaviour in any given set of circumstances is going to be difficult. However objective the theory, the court is going to have to make a subjective assessment of behaviour. In fairness, it is difficult to see how it could be otherwise as the concept of negligence is not, of course, restricted to employers' liability but covers every aspect of human activity. Many other judicial attempts have been made to define negligence. But they are all based on the reasonable man concept and add little. After all, the reasonable man, like the average man (who has rather less than two legs), does not exist.

In the past, it has been customary in employers' liability to try to clarify the general principle by reducing the reasonableness concept to an obligation comprising three "subtorts"; failure to select proper and competent persons to supervise the work; failure to provide adequate materials and resources for the work; and failure to provide a safe system of working. But this approach is not really much help. All that it means is that any of these three failures may be negligent and give rise to liability. And, at any rate, as is explained later at p. 123, this approach is now obsolete and misleading. One judicial attempt, however, seems to have reduced this concept of reasonableness to manageable proportions. It is still based on "reasonable" behaviour, but the way in which it has been formulated seems to provide an acceptable matrix. A New Zealand judge (Callan, J., in *Fletcher Construction Co. Ltd.* v. *Webster* (1948) N2 HC) posed the problem as three questions. Slightly paraphrased they are:

(a) What dangers should an employer foresee if he exercises reasonable foresight?

(b) What remedies should the employer know of for these dangers if he exercised reasonable care and ordinary knowledge?

(c) Are these remedies so expensive or troublesome that the employer is entitled to reject them?

Obviously these three questions also embody a great

number of vague concepts, but they do succeed in defining the problem in a more concrete fashion. So, if the answer to question (*a*) is "none" then you go no further; there is no negligence. The same applies to question (*b*). And, even if there are positive answers to the first two questions, if the answer to question (*c*) is "yes" then there is no negligence.

These three questions need detailed examination:

(*a*) *What dangers should an employer foresee if he exercises reasonable foresight?*

If the answer to this question is "none" then that is an end to the matter. If no danger is foreseeable then there can be no negligence. Is he an optimist or a pessimist? A lion or a mouse? The answer seems to be that something is foreseeable if it can be anticipated by anyone who takes the trouble to sit down and think about any given situation. This is well illustrated by the case of *Carmarthenshire County Council* v. *Lewis* (1955) HL.

> A small boy of four was a pupil at a nursery school run by the County Council. One of the teachers had got him ready to go for a walk with another child. She then left the two children on their own in a classroom whilst she went off to get ready herself. While she was out of the room she met another child who had cut himself. Bandaging the other child and getting ready herself took about ten minutes. While she was away the first boy wandered out of the school on to a busy road where he caused a lorry to swerve and run into a telegraph pole. The driver was killed.

The question of whether this sequence of events was foreseeable was very carefully examined by the House of Lords, especially by Lord Reid:

> "Was it foreseeable by an ordinary reasonable and careful person that a child might sometimes be left alone in the nursery school for a short period? I think it was. I see nothing very extraordinary in the circumstances which caused these children to be left alone. Was it, then, fore-

seeable that such a child might not sit still but might move out of the classroom? If I am right in my view that it is not safe to make assumptions about the behaviour of even young children, again I think it was. Was it then foreseeable that such a child might go into the street, there being no obstacle in its way? I see no ground for assuming that such a child would stay in an empty playground when the gate was not more than twenty yards or so from the classroom. And once the child was in the street anything might happen. It was argued that it might be reasonable to foresee injury to the child but not reasonable to foresee that the child's action would cause injury to others. I can see no force in that. One knows that every day people take risks in order to save others from being run over, and if a child runs into the street the danger to others is almost as great as the danger to the child."

Lord Reid is not, of course, indulging in an exercise in strict logic. If anything his approach is homespun and simple. He shows that, as suggested above, had anybody sat down and thought about what might happen when the child was left they could quite easily have anticipated each stage in the actual sequence of events. But it must also be remembered, despite the objectivity with which Lord Reid cloaks his reasoning, that the courts operate on a basis of hindsight. There will necessarily have been an accident and an injury before the case is heard. This injury will inevitably predispose the court to an analysis of the situation by which the accident could have been foreseen. The reference to optimists and pessimists above was not entirely frivolous. There will always be a tendency towards a pessimistic assessment of probabilities. This "bias" of the court is important in other ways, see p. 144.

In an industrial situation this type of reasoning may seem a little hard. It is unlikely that, even presupposing the inclination, someone in authority is going to sit down to consider each industrial operation and say: "Can somebody for whom we are responsible be injured in normal circumstances on this machine, or doing this job, or in this situation?" Yet this is the criterion that will be applied after the accident has happened. The answer that injury is "unlikely" is not sufficient justification for continuing the state of affairs. Perhaps this is one of the true functions of the safety officer?

However, the liability of the employer is not absolute. There are limits to what he can be expected to foresee. A recent case in the Court of Appeal gives an indication of the frontiers of his liability.

A boring operation was being carried out on a lathe. The chuck revolved at about 30 r.p.m. but the boring bar moved so slowly that, to all intents and purposes, it could be regarded as standing still. The end of the boring bar came to within $\frac{3}{8}''$ to $\frac{1}{2}''$ of the revolving workpiece. No guard was provided for the potential trap between the workpiece and the boring bar but it was far out of reach of the operator. Nevertheless, the operator did manage to get his hand into this trap and three fingers were amputated. How the accident happened was never really established. The plaintiff had his own story but the court rejected it as untrue. They then went on to say that although the plaintiff had been injured the defence had shown that it was so unlikely a happening that such an injury must be considered as completely unforeseeable. The answer to Callan, J.'s first question was, therefore, "none" and there was no negligence on the part of the employer.

Johnson v. *F. E. Callow (Engineers) Ltd.* (1969) CA

An experienced carpenter was fixing nails in concrete lintels using a cartridge assisted hammer. The use of this very noisy tool made him completely deaf in one ear. The court held that the employer was not negligent as, *in the state of knowledge of the "reasonable employer" at the time*, such an injury was not foreseeable. A British Standard Specification which dealt with noise hazards in these tools was published after the injury but before the trial. The judge indicated that had it been available *before* the injury the result might have been different.

Down v. *Dudley, Coles, Long Ltd.* (1969) Devon Assizes

(b) What remedies should the employer know of?

Even if the reasonable employer can foresee dangers, there is no negligence if the answer to this second question is "none". The law of negligence is never prohibitory: only compensatory. Statute may prohibit and prohibit absolutely; the common law of negligence never. It will only compensate for an injury that has been suffered. So, at common law, there is no prohibition on the use of white phosphorus in matches, only compensation for the unfortunate victims of "fossy-jaw"; and that only if it can be shown that there are methods available to protect the worker against the use of the substance. On the other hand, s. 67 of the Factories Act 1961 prohibit the use of the substance absolutely for matchmaking.

It follows, therefore, that the employer is perfectly at liberty to create an intrinsically unsafe situation and to work people in that situation without liability if he can show that there is no remedy for the hazards that he himself has deliberately created. No available remedy means no negligence. Some other legal systems have developed a concept of "ultra-hazardous activities" involving absolute liabilities, but there is no such concept in English law. All that is required where risks are high is an equally high degree of care in using such remedies as are available.

Nor will the knowledge of remedies that the employer ought to have be pushed too far. "Ordinary" knowledge is what is required.

> A surgeon was alleged to have been negligent because he failed to use a new instrument to assist him in diagnosis. It was shown, however, that, although this instrument was used in the United States it was very difficult to obtain here and English surgeons did not normally use it. He was held not to have been negligent.
>
> *Whiteford* v. *Hunter* (1950) HL

In industry the requirements of "ordinary knowledge" will normally be satisfied if the employer follows "general and approved practice" in the industry or trade in question.

When the lowest "lift" of a scaffold used in building operations was about to be dismantled, a charge-hand ordered
the removal of a guard-rail which had been erected for
the protection of workmen on a ledge twenty feet above
the ground. A workman walking along the ledge to help
in the dismantling of the scaffold fell into the street below
and was injured. The employers were able to show that
the removal of the guard-rail at that stage of the proceedings was normal practice in dealing with scaffolding and
they were held not to have been negligent.

Sexton v. *Scaffolding (Great Britain) Ltd.* (1952) CA

Sexton's case hinged, of course, on a special practice in a specific industry. How are special practices proved? Obviously,
of course, expert witnesses play a part. But at least as important are codes of practice produced by industries themselves
and publications of government departments concerned with
questions of safety, health and welfare. So, the electricity
supply industry and the gas industry have produced elaborate
safety codes which they themselves grant almost statutory
status. It is unthinkable that any court would refuse to accept
compliance with such a code as constituting "general and
approved practice". Incidentally, it must be remembered that
such a code works both ways. Anything that was done within
an industry that did not comply with their own code would
almost certainly be regarded as negligence. The authors
believe as well, though they have no direct judicial authority
as yet, that a similar status would be granted by the courts
to any seriously considered and properly drafted "works rules"
even if produced for a single workplace. Clearly care in the
production of such a document is of great importance from
both aspects of its possible use.

In the absence of, or supplementary to, a code of practice,
the instructions and general information disseminated by the
Factory Department and other similar government departments is the most important source of "ordinary knowledge".
Also, in general terms, statutory requirements designed to
cover situations analogous to those in which injury has been
suffered but not covered by them will be accepted as giving

a guide, though arbitrary details of such regulations will not be applied. So Regulation 26 of the Construction (Working Places) Regulations requires that every working platform from which a person is liable to fall 6′ 6″ or more shall be a minimum of 25″ wide. This figure of 25″ will *not* be accepted by the courts as necessary in situations where there are similar working platforms not covered by the regulations. It is an arbitrary figure and will be treated as such. It may, however, be looked at by the courts as an indication of a suitable minimum width in such circumstances.

Finally, the courts will always reserve to themselves the right to condemn even a universal practice in an industry as inadequate and, therefore, negligent. Though they make use of this power very rarely.

> Where a 'bus crashed because of a burst tyre, even though the 'bus company was able to show that they had followed established practice, they were held liable because the House of Lords thought that practice inadequate. The company had not instructed their drivers to report incidents which might cause an unusual type of tyre fracture.
>
> *Barkway* v. *South Wales Transport Co. Ltd.* (1950) HL

(c) *Was the remedy unreasonably expensive or troublesome?*

The common law is concerned with the cost and trouble of dealing with hazards. This is in contrast with obligations under statute, see p. 159. The employer is entitled to claim that the remedy he undoubtedly knows of for the hazard that he can undoubtedly see is too expensive or troublesome to be used. There is a sort of sliding scale. Where any particular situation falls on this scale must be a matter of opinion for decision by the court. The extremes may be easy to point out; the intermediate points not so simple. So, Lord Reid said in the case of *Paris* v. *Stepney Borough Council* (1951) HL:

> "There are occupations in which the possibility of an accident occurring to a workman is extremely remote,

while there are other occupations in which there is a
constant risk of accident. Similarly, there are occupations
in which, if an accident occurs, it is likely to be of a
trivial nature, whilst there are other occupations in
which . . . the result . . . may well be fatal. There is
in each case a gradually ascending scale between the two
extremes . . . the more serious the damage which will
happen if an accident occurs, the more thorough are the
precautions which an employer must take."

Perhaps one day some brave man will graph the curves of
possible injury against the cost of remedy, thus defining the
area of liability. For the moment each case must be taken
on its merits.

A factory was flooded by exceptionally heavy rain which
left a slippy mixture of cooland and water on the floor
when it drained away. The employer had to make a
decision as to whether to close the whole factory or to
continue working taking such precautions as he could.
In this case putting sawdust on the floor. The employer
chose to keep the factory open and, almost inevitably, a
man slipped and broke his leg. The House of Lords
rejected the necessity for closing the factory as being an
unreasonable burden taken in conjunction with the nature
of the risk.

Latimer v. *AEC Ltd.* (1953) HL

It will be noted that the injury here was only a broken leg.
Bearing in mind, yet again, that the courts have the benefit
of hindsight, one wonders whether the result would have been
the same had the employee been killed. As he might well
have been had he struck his head against something in falling.
   Paris's case above illustrates another important aspect of
liability which does not fit conveniently under any of the
heads set out by Callan, J. The case concerned a one-eyed
workman who lost his only good eye at work in rather exceptional circumstances. The House of Lords held that Paris's
employers were under an obligation to take more care of the

single eye than of any one eye of a two-eyed man. This case, and the many variations possible upon it, raises the whole question of peculiarities of individual employees. How far is the employer required to make provision for them? The answer is now quite clear: the employer is required to take special precautions in respect of the individual disabilities of employees if he knows about them or ought to have known about them. "Ought to have known" does not yet mean, at common law, that the employer is under an obligation to seek out any mental or physical deficiencies in his employees by medical examination or otherwise (though he may be required to do this by statute in certain cases). In practice many employers do this, but it is at least seriously arguable that it puts them in a worse position in respect of employers' liability than those employers who do not. Probably the most important aspect of "ought to have known" is that if any member of the management of an organisation (even a charge-hand) knows of the disability, this knowledge will be imputed to the employer, who must, therefore, accept responsibility.

> A workman lost his eye when a piece flew off a badly hardened chisel. The charge-hand knew that the chisel was defective. This was sufficient to impute the knowledge to the company.
>
> *Taylor* v. *Rover* (1966) Birmingham Assizes

It is clear that, even helped by the sort of analysis used above, the concept of negligence is more simple in theory than in practice. There are serious difficulties in attempting to forecast the result of any set of facts. The jury was a useful tool of analysis. "Reasonableness" is so often remote from true human behaviour and the strength of the jury was their willingness at times to be utterly unreasonable themselves. We no longer have juries in negligence cases. It all depends upon which way the judicial cat decides to jump.

III   BREACH OF STATUTORY DUTY

Where duties are imposed by a statute which is intended to benefit a class of the community, a member of that class may have a right to an action for damages if he is injured as a result of a failure to carry out the duty. This right is known as an action for breach of statutory duty.

This right is not merely "statutory negligence" (though see p. 135): it is a separate right of action with its own rules. Its scope is defined not by the common law (though it is a common law action) but by the terms of the statute upon which it is based. As statutes such as the Factories Act and the Mines and Quarries Act (and especially the statutory regulations made under these acts) are normally fairly precise in their requirements this often makes the action for breach of statutory duty a more attractive proposition than that of negligence. In practice the two forms of action are used in the alternative: an action for breach of the statute *and* negligence. Thus, if the more precise action fails, recourse can be had to the greater vagueness of the action for negligence.

Whether or not a statute gives a right to an action such as this is a matter of statutory interpretation. Usually modern protective statutes do so but not always. So, if a person employed in a factory is injured on an unfenced dangerous part of machinery there is no doubt that he has a right to an action for breach of statutory duty. If, however, the same person is injured because of failure to maintain fire escapes as required by the London Building Acts it is by no means clear that an action for breach of the statute is available (*Solomons* v. *R. Gertzenstein Ltd.* (1954) CA). And even in the case of the Factories Act not all the provisions will give the right to an action on the statute. Some merely place obligations on the employer backed by criminal sanctions. So, s. 17 of the Act of 1961 stipulates certain standards of fencing for new machinery. The courts have held that an action for breach of statutory duty does not lie under that section. It is all a matter of interpretation and each section of an Act will be looked at individually even after the courts have decided that the Act as a whole falls into the category of statutes that, prima facie, give rise to such an action.

However, it is now well established that most of the important sections of what might be called the "standard" protective Acts give a right to an action under them.

As in the case of negligence the action for breach of statutory duty is best approached by a number of deceptively simple questions:

(i) Does the statute apply?
(ii) Is the person injured one of the class of persons that the statute is intended to protect?
(iii) Is there a breach of the statute?
(iv) Was the injury caused by the breach?
(v) On whom does the liability fall?

As before, each of these questions needs amplification.

(i) *Does the statute apply?*

The application of most protective statutes is defined by reference to the place of work. The definition is contained within the statute itself and is often long and complex. For example, s. 175 of the Factories Act 1961 defines the term "factory". The section alone runs to more than 1,000 words. If the judicial gloss were added then it would be possible to write a substantial book upon the meaning of the word "factory" alone. Fortunately the complexity of the definition arises not out of the run-of-the-mill cases but out of the inevitable borderline situations which have to be provided for in the statute and which, despite all the care that the draftsman may lavish, still give rise to problems of interpretation. In 999 cases out of every 1000 it is quite plain whether or not the premises are a factory and, therefore, whether the Act applies. Precisely the same position arises in the case of the Offices, Shops and Railway Premises Act, the Mines and Quarries Act and all similar legislation. The problem of the definition of the premises subject to various acts is dealt with in some detail at p. 164.

At the risk of stating the obvious it is clear that if the

statute does not apply there can be no action for breach of statutory duty, however analogous the work-situation may be to one covered by the statute:

> A water board occupied an area of 64 acres. There were various buildings including a filter house and a pump house which were physically separated. An employee was seriously injured in the pump house. The Court held that the filter house was a factory but the pump house was not: no "factory process" was carried on there as nothing was done to the water other than pumping it.
>
> *Longhurst* v. *Guildford, Godalming and District Water Board* (1961) HL

(ii) *Is the injured person protected?*

As stated above, the application of protective statutes is usually defined by premises. It might be logical to assume that any person lawfully on those premises would get the benefit of the statute. But this is not the case. To take the Factories Act as the prime example, there is even variation from one section of the Act to another as to who is entitled to protection. In s. 14 (fencing machinery) it is "any person employed or working on the premises"; in s. 76 (regulations) it is "persons employed" without the addition of the words "or working". In s. 29 (safe access) the words used are "any person", but the section then goes on to limit its application to a place where "any person" "has to work"; this seems to be equivalent to "persons working"?

In addition to the variations in drafting, judicial interpretation had played a part in confusing the issue:

> A fireman fighting a fire in a factory was refused the protection of the Act because he was not, in the court's opinion, a "person employed" in the factory within the meaning of s. 76. The employment has to be for the direct purposes of the factory.
>
> *Hartley* v. *Mayoh Ltd.* (1954) CA

It must be stressed yet again that this is a problem that must not be overemphasised. In most cases the application of the statute is clear. But it must always be looked at in conjunction with any limiting words such as above in case any particular should lie on the borderline or even clearly outside it.

(iii) *Is there a breach of the statute?*

This is, also, a matter of statutory interpretation; it depends on the words of the statute. But, once more, the vast majority of cases, despite occasional judicial abberations, fall quite clearly on one side of the line or the other. This is one of the advantages of the action upon the statute as opposed to the action for negligence. What is more, many statutory obligations are "absolute", *i.e.* the mere fact that the thing prohibited happens is enough to bring about a breach. Intention, knowledge, cost of compliance are all irrelevant. Section 22 of the Factories Act requires that "every hoist or lift shall be of good mechanical construction, sound material and adequate strength and shall be properly maintained". These words have many times been held to create an "absolute" obligation on the employer. If a hoist or lift fails there is a breach of the Act irrespective of the reason and it is no defence to prove that there was no ascertainable cause for the failure or that the failure happened despite an efficient system of inspection and maintenance. The defence of "good and approved practice" is useless here. The statute stipulates its own practice and its own standards. If they are impossibly high at times there is nothing that can be done about it.

Of course not all statutory requirements are as stringent as those quoted above. Many involve considerations of "practicability" and "reasonableness". But, despite their less stringent nature, they are, in one sense at least, still "absolute". Even though some such phrase as "so far as may be reasonably practicable" may have modified the absolute nature of the obligation, the duty to observe it is absolute and cannot be avoided by any means.

(iv) *Was the injury caused by the breach*?

At this stage it is sufficient to say that some causal connection must be shown between the breach of the statute and the injury, though certain rather more sophisticated aspects of causation will have to be considered later, see p. 149.

The breach of the statute need not have been the *sole* cause of the injury. If A slips on a banana skin at work and falls against an unfenced part of machinery which injures him there are, in any normal usage of the word, two "causes": the banana skin and the unfenced machinery. This in no way affects the fact that the breach of the statute was *a* cause and that there can be liability.

The causal connection must be foreseeable using precisely the same tests as those given above in the case of negligence. What is more, the courts are always ready to infer a causal connection where an injury is suffered which is clearly of the type envisaged by the protective legislation, even where there is no evidence to show how the injury was sustained. The courts will not concern themselves greatly with causal connections when a man is found beside his machine with his head chopped off:

> A workman fell off a scaffold which did not comply with the Building Regulations. Unknown to his employers he was an epileptic and his fall was a result of a fit. Nevertheless the employers were held 50 per cent to blame as a properly equipped scaffold *might* have stopped him falling.
>
> *Cork* v. *Kirby Maclean Ltd.* (1952) CA

(v) *Whose is the liability*?

In general, protective statutes do not operate in terms of "employers". The Factories Act, the Offices, Shops and Railway Premises Act and the Occupiers' Liability Act all operate through the "occupier" of the factory, office or other premises. In most cases the "occupier" will also be the "employer", but it need not necessarily be so: a non-servant may have an action against the occupier of a factory when he is working there as a contractor on behalf of someone else. In an extreme case the receiver and manager for debenture holders was held to be the "occupier" though he was certainly not the employer (*Meigh* v. *Wickenden* (1942) DC).

IV STATUTORY NEGLIGENCE

The definition of employers' liability given above (p. 121) refers only to negligence and breach of statutory duty. This is an accurate and exhaustive description, but there are two anomalous situations where breach of a statute may give rise not to an action for breach of statutory duty but to an action for negligence: "statutory negligence". As both these statutes are of considerable practical importance they merit a brief special treatment. The two statutes are the Occupiers' Liability Act 1957 and the Employers' Liability (Defective Equipment) Act 1969.

Occupiers' Liability Act 1957

Like most other protective legislation this Act is concerned with premises and their occupation. The common law developed a complex set of rules regarding obligations of occupiers of premises to visitors to them. They were categorised as "invitees", "licensees" and "trespassers". The distinction between an invitee and a licensee became so fine and the cases on the point so irreconcilable that this Act was passed in an attempt to sort out the mess. The Act abolishes the old distinction between invitees and licensees, considering them both merely as persons lawfully on the premises. The remaining classification of trespasser is untouched by the act.

The term "occupier" is not defined but relates, as does, say, the similar term in the Factories Act, to control. There may be more than one occupier, in which case their liabilities will depend upon the *degree* of control enjoyed by each. In the industrial situation there is not likely to be any serious problem as to joint occupiers.

The Act imposes an obligation on the occupier to see that the visitor (including his own employees) will be reasonably safe in using the premises for the purposes for which he is invited or permitted to be there. This obligation includes dangers from the work going on and not merely dangers arising from the premises as such (*Savory* v. *Holland Hannen & Cubitts (Southern) Ltd.* (1964) CA). But a person who is on the premises to exercise his calling is expected to appreciate and guard against any risks arising out of it so far as the occupier allows him to do so. Warning notices are not sufficent.

Until the recent case of *British Railways Board* v. *Herrington* (1972) HL, an occupier was under no liability to a trespasser in respect of his premises. If the roof fell on the trespasser's head he had no right of action. The occupier's sole liability was not to set in motion, wilfully or recklessly, anything that might do harm to a trespasser that the occupier knew, or ought to have known, to be present:

> A small boy of six was playing with two elder brothers on National Trust property. From the field a path ran to an electrified railway line. The line was protected by a 4' chain link fence, but at one point it had been pushed down to within 10" of the ground. This gap was frequently used as a short cut across the line. The Board knew of this. The child went through the gap and was injured on the live rail. The House held that the Board were liable. When, they said, an occupier knows, or ought to know, that there are trespassers on his land and also knows of physical facts in relation to his land that would be a serious danger to persons not knowing of them, then he must regulate his behaviour "by standards of common sense and common humanity".

British Railways Board v. *Herrington* (1972) HL

What this new standard of care means will take some time to elucidate. Clearly, it is a lesser standard than that of the reasonable man but one might have thought that "common sense" and "common humanity" were precisely the attributes that the reasonable man might be expected to have.

Employers' Liability (Defective Equipment) Act 1969

The law of employers' liability developed, of course, in the nineteenth century. The social climate of that time, which was largely shared by the judges, was employer-orientated. This led to many unsatisfactory developments (see, for example, the comments on contributory negligence and *volenti* at pp. 147–149) which, in their turn as the social climate changed, had to be evaded. These days it is difficult to "change" the common law. The courts prefer a more crabwise approach.

One of the more unfortunate developments was the concept of "common employment". This meant that an employee could not sue his employer for injuries received at work as a result of the negligence of a fellow-servant; even a superior servant such as a manager. The employer was liable only for his "personal" negligence. So far as third parties were concerned the doctrine of "vicarious liability" applied: see p. 141.

As industry became more complex, and with the great increase of corporations which had only a "fictional" personality, common employment obviously presented a serious hardship to the employee. The judges at last realised that they had to try and find a way around the problem they had created.

One result was the judicial development of the concept of various artificial "personal" obligations of the employer. As set out in the famous case of *Wilsons & Clyde Coal Co. Ltd.* v. *English* (1937) HL there were three: to select proper and competent persons to superintend the work; to furnish adequate materials and resources for the work; and to provide a proper system of working.

The Law Reform (Personal Injuries) Act 1948 did away with common employment and, therefore, with the need for the "personal" obligations. This new freedom was reflected in the case of *Davie* v. *New Merton Board Mills Ltd.* (1959) HL.

> The employer had bought a "drift" (a sort of oversized chisel) from a reputable supplier. It was defective. On the basis of the three "personal" duties quoted above, the employer would have been liable to the employee injured as a result of the defect. He, the employer, had

failed to provide adequate materials and resources for the work. The House of Lords rejected this view. They held that the source of the employer's liability was negligence the same as anyone else's and that, in buying tools from a reputable supplier, the employers had not been negligent.

In many ways this decision was fair enough, but there may well be occasions when it would lead to hardship. The suppliers of the tools might no longer exist when the injury was suffered. The Act of 1969 therefore reverses the decision in *Davie* (though the reasoning is not affected). It is rather oddly drafted:

"Where...
   (*a*) an employee suffers personal injury in the course of his employment in consequence of a defect of equipment provided by his employer for the purposes of the employer's business; and
   (*b*) the defect is attributable wholly or partly to the fault of a third party (whether identified or not)
the injury shall be deemed to be also attributable to negligence on the part of the employer . . ."

"Fault" is defined as negligence, breach of statutory duty or any other tort; "equipment" is defined as including any plant and machinery, vehicle, aircraft and clothing.

The short extract above is virtually the whole of the effective part of the Act. It will be seen that liability is still based on negligence. This time at one remove. The employer is negligent because some other person is negligent. As was pointed out above, one of the main objections to *Davie* was the possible hardship that might result to employees who were left only with an action against a supplier or manufacturer. The latter might be bankrupt, non-existent (shut down) or difficult to sue (foreign manufacturer). Obviously these situations will be almost as difficult under the new Act. The problems of *proof* of some other party's negligence will on occasion be quite serious. Much will depend on the attitude that the courts take to the interpretation of the Act and the standard of proof of negligence that they require. Possibly they will operate largely on the basis of *res ipsa loquitur* (see p. 144). If they do not it is a little difficult to see how the Act can function.

There is, of course, nothing to prevent the employer from including an indemnity against any liability under the Act in any contract of sale or hire of "equipment" that he enters into.

V   THE SCOPE OF EMPLOYERS' LIABILITY

So far the *nature* of employers' liability has been discussed. It derives from negligence (including the two examples of "statutory negligence") and breach of statutory duty. But what is the *scope* of the liability? To whom and for whom is the employer liable because of his status as employer?

To whom is the Employer Liable?

As an employer the liability is to his servants and only to them. The employer may be liable to non-servants, but it is never in his capacity as employer. So the occupier of premises may be liable to non-servants under the provisions of a statute. But it is as an occupier that he is liable, not as an employer, though he may well be both.

The only problems that arise are those concerned with "volunteer workers" and even those are not difficult to solve.

Suppose A sees B, C and D, who are all servants of Z, doing a job of work and in difficulties. He volunteers to help them. A piece of equipment supplied by Z for his servants' use is defective and breaks. A is seriously injured. Has he a right of action against Z? The answer, quite simply, depends on whether A became a servant or not whilst he was helping B, C and D. As was pointed out in Chapter 2, remuneration is not a necessary element in the master–servant relationship. Whether A became a temporary servant is, therefore, a matter of law for the court to decide on the criteria set out in that chapter. If he did then he is in exactly the same position as any other servant. If he did not then he is in exactly the same position as any other non-servant.

For whom is the Employer Liable?

It must be remembered that most employers are corporations. They exist only as legal fictions. Liability for their personal actions is, therefore, meaningless except where the term "personal" is given an artificial meaning as it was in *Wilsons & Clyde Coal Co. Ltd.* v. *English* above. And even when the employer is a natural person the complexity of employment may be such that much has to be done through his agents and servants. It is fair and reasonable, therefore, that the employer's liability should extend beyond the confines of the results of his—or its—personal actions or defaults and include equal liability for the acts or defaults of others who are acting on his behalf. This extension of liability is known as "vicarious liability".

An employer is vicariously liable for the negligence or breach of statutory duty committed by his servants in the course of their duties. So, if A employs B as a van-driver he is liable for the negligent driving of the van if a third party is injured by it. It is of no concern that B drives the van in some way that A has specifically forbidden. A is liable because B has been negligent in doing the job that he was employed to do. The fact that he was doing it badly is irrelevant: A must still accept vicarious liability.

Obviously problems will arise as to what acts are performed within the scope of the duties and what outside. The dividing line will be very shadowy on occasion; especially when the tortious act has been done in contravention of orders. It is impossible to rationalise the many decisions illustrating the course of the servant's duties and they are, at any rate, special to the individual case. But, so far as failure to comply with orders is concerned, it is reasonably accurate to say that breaches of orders which limit the *scope* of the employment take the servant outside the course of his duties. Breach of an order that merely regulates the *manner* in which the servant carries out his job does not.

> A servant who lit a cigarette whilst pouring petrol from a drum to a tin was acting in the course of his duties.
>
> *Jefferson* v. *Derbyshire Farmers* (1921) KB

So was one pouring petrol from a vehicle into a tank.

Century Insurance Co. Ltd. v. *Northern Ireland R.T.B.* (1942) HL

Where a servant specifically ordered not to give lifts did so and the passenger was injured, the employer was held not liable on the rather doubtful grounds that the servant was outside the scope of his employment.

Conway v. *George Wimpey Ltd.* (1951) CA

Rather more difficult to explain are the circumstances in which an employer will be vicariously liable for the tortious acts of non-servants. As was explained in Chapter 2, a servant is someone who works for a master under a contract of service. Whether or not a contract is of service is largely determined by a combination of the "control" test and the "integration" test. Plus various additional factual factors: who pays the "servant", who has the right to dismiss and so on. The result is that you can have the servant of A working for B on loan with no contractual relationship at all. So, though to all except a lawyer the employee would appear to be B's servant, in law he cannot be.

An unskilled labourer (Clegg) was loaned by his employers (Eastwoods) to a firm of contractors (Le Grand). Clegg's consent was not asked for by Eastwoods; he was just sent. In the course of his work for Le Grand he was killed through the admitted negligence of one of their servants. Le Grand had two insurance policies with different companies. One covered personal injury by accident to "any person under a contract of service". The sole question in the case was which of the two insurance companies should pay. The Court of Appeal held that Clegg was at all times the servant of his original masters Eastwoods. The fact that Le Grand had the temporary right to control Clegg's actions did not affect this. All three judges, however, said that they considered that had Clegg been the person who had been negligent and some third party killed, Le Grand would have been vicariously liable for his negligence. For the purposes of vicarious liability Clegg had become what might be called a "pseudo-servant". This had come about by the degree of control that Le Grand were exercising over him at the time. As Lord Denning said: "If a temporary employer has the right to control the manner in which a labourer does his work, so as to be able to tell him the right way or the wrong way to do it, then he should be responsible when he does it in the wrong way as well as in the right way. The right of control carries with it the burden of responsibility."

Denham v. *Midland Employers Mutual Assurance Ltd.* (1955) CA

The position with regard to non-servants appears to be, therefore, that if he satisfies the "control" test *or* the "integration" test then, even in the absence of any of the other necessary factors to make him a servant, he becomes a pseudo-servant and the employer is vicariously liable for his torts.

An excellent example of the pseudo-servant situation is given by the quite complicated case of *Sumner* v. *William Henderson & Sons Ltd.* (1964) QB:

The defendants were owners of a large store that was being modernised. The store business was being carried on whilst the work was being done. An electric cable had to be laid from one floor to another. The cable was obtained from a manufacturer to specifications given by consultant engineers. It was installed by electrical contractors in accordance with the plans of and under the supervision of architects. A fire broke out in the premises due either to a fault in the cable or in its installation and an employee of the defendants was killed. The judge had an unusual number of contractors to deal with and he sorted them out in respect of liability as suggested above. The defendants could not be vicariously liable for the suppliers of the cable. That was a *Davie* situation: buying a cable was no different from buying a tool over the counter of a shop. (Since the Employers' Liability

(Defective Equipment) Act 1969 the situation may be different, see p. 138.) But, as the business of the store was being carried on whilst the work was being done, the rest of the contractors working in the store must be regarded as integrated into the working of the store for the time being and the defendants were, therefore, liable for their negligence.

VI   PRESUMPTION AGAINST THE EMPLOYER

The law in action operates on the basis of presumptions. They are used as a starting point for litigation. This is not necessary. Each case could start in a vacuum of non-presumption with the court equally open to persuasion from either side. But English law prefers to start with a presumption one way or the other. The best known of these presumptions is, of course, the presumption of innocence in criminal cases; the accused is presumed to be innocent until he is proved guilty. An example of a specialised presumption that operates in civil cases was given in Chapter 2: any restraint of trade clause in a contract of service is presumed to be void as against public policy. It is the task of the person trying to enforce the restraint to show that it is reasonable and therefore enforceable.

The importance of the presumption is that it shifts the burden of proof. The prosecution in a criminal case bear this burden. If they offer no evidence then the accused must be acquitted. But every case starts with the burden of proof on one side or the other. It is normal to quote the saying "he who alleges must prove", but the example of restraint quoted above shows that in fact this is not so.

An important presumption so far as negligence is concerned is expressed in the Latin tag *res ipsa loquitur*: "the matter speaks for itself". As one judge explained it:

"... where the thing is shown to be under the management of the defendant ... and the accident is such as in the ordinary course of things does not happen if those who have the management use proper care, it affords reasonable evidence, in the absence of explanation by the defendant, that the accident arose from want of care".

Erle, C. J., in *Scott* v. *London Dock Co.* (1865) Ex Ch

In fact this important maxim has been used very sparingly by the courts. It has been restricted largely to cases where, from the nature of the facts, evidence has been very hard to obtain: explosions, objects falling from above, etc. The reason for care in its use is obvious. If the presumption is adopted then the other side bears the burden of proof. If no evidence is available then the burden is almost impossible to discharge. It is not suggested that there has been any increase in the use of the *res ipsa* concept in recent years, but a new presumption, as yet unadmitted by the courts but, on analysis, clearly present, seems to have grown up. This presumption, too, could be expressed conveniently in a maxim: *noxa ipsa loquitur*: "the injury speaks for itself". So much so that it seems by now quite clear that every employers' liability case starts with a presumption of liability on the part of the employer once the fact of injury has been shown.

In a recent case brought for breach of statutory duty under s. 29(1) of the Factories Act 1961 (see Chapter 10) an employee was hurt when a ladder slipped despite having been fitted with suction pads. The Court of Appeal held that the employers were liable. The employers could exculpate themselves only by showing that they had taken all reasonable precautions to make the ladder safe. They had, in fact, advanced no evidence and had, therefore, failed to discharge their burden of proof. This was a clear case of the presumption operating against the employer. In theory the onus was on the plaintiff to show that the employer had not taken reasonable care; if he failed to do so then theoretically he must lose his case. In fact, all the plaintiff proved was what had happened: the ladder had slipped and he had been injured. But the Court then required a satisfactory explanation from the employer. As it was not offered, the employer was liable.

Garner v. *John Thompson (Wolverhampton) Ltd.* (1968) CA

Precisely the same approach was taken in another recent case in rather more complex circumstances. A seaman was badly scalded when he turned on a showerbath in the crew's quarters of a ship and the water came out at at least 150°F. Special Regulations required the provision of thermostatic control to prevent this. But, quite apart from the Regulations, the judge held that the employers were negligent even though the plaintiff did nothing more than prove what had happened. The *reason* for the water being scalding was never discovered. Once again, in the absence of any satisfactory explanation to the contrary, and with no real evidence at all, the employer was liable.

Foulder v. *Canadian Pacific Steam Ships Ltd.* (1969) Liverpool Summer Assizes

As an employers' liability case presupposes injury to an employee this means that every case will start with a presumption that the injured person is entitled to recover damages. It is up to the employer to rebut this presumption.

The law of employers' liability is, therefore, the law of the *defences* available to the employer.

VII DEFENCES AVAILABLE TO THE EMPLOYER

The employer has four defences available to him, the last of which can also be subdivided into four:

1   That there was no negligence or breach of statutory duty.
2   That even if there were negligence or breach of statutory duty, the person injured did not fall into the

class of those protected by these common law
duties.
3   *Volenti non fit injuria.*
4   Lack of causal connection. This can be subdivided
into:
    (*a*) contributory neglegence;
    (*b*) "sole cause";
    (*c*) "hypothetical causes";
    (*d*) remoteness.

The nature of negligence and breach of statutory duty was
explained earlier in this chapter. The defence to accusations
that these torts have been committed is explicit in that
explanation. The other defences, however, need detailed examination.

Volenti non fit injuria

This Latin maxim means that if a person voluntarily sub-
jects himself to a particular type of risk, he has no right of
action if he suffers injury from that risk.

In the nineteenth century the plea of "*volenti*" was one of
the employers' main defences in employers' liability cases. The
employee was presumed to have contractually accepted all the
risks of his employment that he knew of, or ought to have
known of, when he entered into the contract. This acceptance
was deemed to apply even to breaches of statutory requirements. But, as a general defence, the famous case of *Smith*
v. *Baker* (1891) HL killed it. And the equally important but
lesser known case of *Baddely* v. *Earl Granville* (1867) QBD
decided that it was not available in the case of an action for
breach of statutory duty.

The unsatisfactory nature of the defence is implicit in the
very maxim itself. The action is for negligence. How often
can anyone be said to be willing to accept another person's
negligence? It may well be that "danger money" or some other
consideration might persuade an employee to accept intrinsically dangerous situations. But as explained above such situations are not part of the law of negligence. And in another
famous judgement Scott, L. J., gave a further cogent reason

for rejecting the concept as a general defence. Freedom of
choice, said the judge, presupposes a lack of pressure. The
very nature of the master–servant relationship makes such a
freedom very unlikely (*Bowater* v. *Rowley Regis Corporation*
(1944) CA).

In the case of breach of statutory duty the validity of the
maxim is even more easily disposed of. In a protective statute
Parliament sets a standard. It would be wrong to allow individuals to contract to depart from that standard. Protective
legislation is intended to protect, sometimes willy-nilly. The
courts will not, therefore, allow the parties to contract out and
any attempt to do so will be void.

Nevertheless the defence still theoretically exists and the
House of Lords have recently invoked it in a manner which
is of some practical importance.

> *ICI* v. *Shatwell* (1965) HL was a shot-firing case. Two
> brothers combined together to break the strict shot-firing
> regulations used by their joint employer. As a result they
> were both injured. One of the brothers sued the
> employer, basing his claim on the negligent act of his
> brother. For this act the employer was, of course, vicar-
> iously liable. It is easy to understand the Court's
> dilemma. Clearly there was little moral merit in the case.
> No doubt the other brother was waiting to present his
> case when the first was successfully concluded. But the
> vicious circle of liability was complete. Each brother was
> 50 per cent to blame for his own injury. The other fifty
> per cent must fall upon the employer. However, the case
> was further complicated by the fact that statutory regula-
> tions placed a duty on the brothers but not on the
> employers. The Court seized upon this complication as
> a way out of their problem. They made new law
> and gave some new life to the *volenti* principle by holding
> that where a statutory duty is placed on the employee
> with no equivalent duty on the employer the defence of
> *volenti* is available in cases where the employer would
> otherwise have been vicariously liable. In this case the
> two brothers were *volens* one another. The employer
> was, therefore, not liable.

At first sight *Shatwell*'s case would only appear to re-establish *volenti* as a defence in very narrow terms. But it has already been followed twice by lower courts in the short period since it was decided. Also it must be remembered that statutes quite often put obligations on employees: sometimes much wider ones than those put on employers. So, s. 143(2) of the Factories Act 1961 stipulates:

> "No person employed in a factory or in any other place to which any provisions of this Act apply shall wilfully and without reasonable cause do anything likely to endanger himself or others."

This is a much wider duty than anything imposed on the employer. The employer's duties are specific: to fence machinery, to provide safe means of access, etc. This wide duty could obviously cover everything from taking off a guard from a machine to throwing stones or riding a motor bike at a dangerous speed through the factory. It will, therefore, easily be seen that the principle of *Shatwell's* case could easily be extended in a factory situation to exculpate the employer in a number of situations for which he might well have expected to bear responsibility.

Lack of Causal Connection

As pointed out earlier, negligence or breach of statutory duty can only be actionable if it was the "cause" of the injury complained of. Suppose that X falls over a badly laid steel plate in a gangway in a factory. He falls down some stairs into a tank of cold water. Three days later he develops pneumonia from which he dies. The badly laid plate was clearly a breach of s. 28 of the Factories Act. But was that breach the cause of his death? Or, again, father and son work for the same employer. The son is killed by the negligence of a third employee. The employer is clearly vicariously liable for this death. The father, who saw the accident happen, broods upon it and eventually commits suicide. Was his son's death the cause of his suicide?

Unfortunately mock-philosophical problems of this kind often come before the courts and lack of causal connection is one of the main defences available to the employer. It is probably convenient to consider them under four heads though, in practice, all four classifications tend to overlap.

(i) *Contributory negligence*

In the harsher days of the nineteenth century, contributory negligence was a complete defence in an action for personal injuries, however trivial the contribution may have been. The Law Reform (Contributory Negligence) Act 1945 changed this hard rule and where an employee is guilty of contributory negligence the court must reduce the amount of the damages in proportion to the employee's share of the responsibility. So, in such a case, damages of £X will be awarded but will be reduced by Y per cent because of the employee's contributory negligence.

Although this defence is truly causal in its nature, the assessment of the percentage by which the award is to be reduced is not calculated on a causal basis but on the criterion of fault. Once some degree of contributory negligence has been established the court will assess the relative *blameworthiness* of the parties and make their apportionment accordingly. The relative degree of *causation* is not considered.

> When a Pakistani labourer chased a pigeon into a part of a factory where he had no right to be and was caught on an unfenced part of machinery that he had no right to be near, his damages were reduced by the trial judge by 80 per cent for contributory negligence. What is more, the Court of Appeal said that the trial judge had been hard on the *employers* in his assessment, though they did not interfere with it. On any sort of causal assessment this was clearly wrong. It is obviously possible to argue that the degree of causation in the actions of the plaintiff was very small indeed. But he had behaved badly and been disobedient and the court, therefore, punished him for it. Which is surely not the function of damages in English law.
>
> *Uddin* v. *Associated Portland Cement Manufacturers Ltd.* (1954) CA

Indeed, in one notorious case Denning, J., held the plaintiff guilty of 100 per cent, contributory negligence despite the contradiction in terms. The plaintiff's blame, he said, ". . . involves a consideration, not only of the causative potency of a particular factor, but also of its blameworthiness" (*Lavender* v. *Diamints Ltd.* (1948) CA).

It is interesting to compare *Uddin's* case with *Laszcsyk* v. *National Coal Board* (1954) Manchester Assizes:

> The plaintiff had, for a long period, been contravening shotfiring regulations and, therefore, had been in breach of statutory duty. But this was done with the knowledge and agreement of his foreman. When he was injured by the negligence of another shotfirer it was quite clear that his own breach of duty was, considered as a matter of causation, a very large degree to blame. Nevertheless the judge reduced his damages by only 5 per cent because the agreement and condonation of his superiors made the plaintiff's blame very little.

The term "negligence" in contributory negligence means the same as it does in the primary negligence concept. Though breach of statutory duty is always "statutory negligence" here. But it must be remembered that what counts is reasonable behaviour in the circumstances in which the worker finds himself. The greatest of modern English judges, Lord Wright, once said that "some carelessness or inattention [by the workman] to his own safety" was not contributory negligence and that we "have to draw the line where mere thoughtlessness or inadvertence or forgetfulness ceases and where negligence begins" (*Caswell* v. *Powell Duffryn Associated Colleries Ltd.* (1940) HL). And where the case is based on breach of statutory duty the difficulties of alleging contributory negligence are still greater. Goddard, L. J., said in the case of *Hutchinson* v. *L.N.E. Rly. Co.* (1942) CA: "I always directed myself to be exceedingly chary of finding contributory negligence where the contributory negligence alleged was the very thing which the statutory duty of the employer was designed to prevent".

The standard of behaviour expected of the industrial worker

is, therefore, theoretically low. (Though in practice it is a little odd that almost every case of complexity sufficient to bring it before the courts ends with some element of contributory negligence being found to exist.) This has been said to result in a rather disconcerting dual standard. The acts of an employee may be "negligence" for the purposes of an action brought by a second employee injured as a result of them. They may not, however, be "negligence" for the purposes of contributory negligence (*Staveley Iron & Chemical Co. Ltd.* v. *Jones* (1956) HL).

(ii) *Sole cause*

Since the case of *Ross* v. *Portland Cement Ltd.* (1964) HL and, more recently, *Boyle* v. *Kodak Ltd.* (1969) HL, it is a little difficult to know how much of this defence is left. But the judges in *Boyle's* case were at pains to point out that it did still exist. It must, therefore, be dealt with as the results to the plaintiff are so catastrophic.

The defence seems to mean that although the employer has been guilty of negligence or breach of statutory duty, the behaviour of the injured employee has been so outrageous that the breach of employer can and must be ignored. At first sight this may appear to be the same approach as that of Denning, J., in *Lavender* v. *Diamints* quoted earlier. And indeed the distinction is a fine one. But the basis of distinction appears to be that "sole cause" is assessed (at least theoretically) on the basis of causation and not on blameworthiness.

> A toolsetter was killed when working on a press. Cantley, J., held that at the time of the accident the press was not guarded as the Factories Act required. Nevertheless the failure of the dead man to carry out the full safety drill as laid down by his employers (and which, in the judge's opinion would have prevented the accident) was so overriding a cause of the accident that the employer's breach of statutory duty could be ignored.
>
> *Horne* v. *Lec Refrigeration* (1965) Sussex Assizes

Set out bluntly like this it may well be that the decision

in *Horne's* case appears too absurd to be true. The very concept of a "sole" cause when, *ex hypothesi*, there must be at least two is vaguely ridiculous.

It is, however, doubtful if *Horne* could be decided the same way today.

> In *Ross's* case quoted above the plaintiff's husband, a chargehand steel-erector, had been killed in a fall from a ladder whilst carrying out an unusual and difficult job with two other men. The men had inadequate equipment but had improvised and got on with the job. They used an obviously unsafe method of work. The defendants for their part were clearly in breach of the Factories Act. Nevertheless at the trial the judge held that as Ross had chosen his own method of work he was the sole cause of his death. What was more (and this distinguishes this situation from that in *Horne* above where a method of work that satisfied the judge as being safe was laid down by the employer) the unsafe method of work used was the cause of the employers being in breach of the Factories Act. The Court of Appeal agreed with the trial judge. The House of Lords, however, unanimously reversed this decision. All five judges stressed that whilst the defence of sole cause could exist, it did so only in very limited situations. Usually only in a clear case of disobedience to adequate and explicit instructions and perhaps only where the injured employee's job was such that some special skill could be expected. They quoted as an example the case of *Ginty* v. *Belmont Building Supplies Ltd.* (1959) QBD where the judge ignored a breach of the Building Regulations on the part of the employers when the plaintiff failed to use crawling boards on a roof in disobedience to express orders.

The scope of the defence appears to have been cut down still further by the recent House of Lords decision in *Boyle* v. *Kodak*. And, in addition, an important piece of new law has been judicially created:

> The plaintiff was an experienced painter who was paint-

ing the outside of a large storage tank. To paint the top
he had to work from a ladder resting on a rail round
the top of the tank. To comply with the employer's obligations under the Building Regulations the ladder had to
be tied at the top. The plaintiff fell when he was climb-
ing the ladder to lash it. In fact he need not have climbed
the ladder to do so as there was an outside staircase
and he could have climbed that and then lashed the
ladder. He had been given no instructions on this point.
By failing to use the staircase the plaintiff was also in
breach of the Building Regulations. At the trial the judge
held that the plaintiff's breach was the sole cause of the
accident and dismissed his claim. The Court of Appeal
took the same view. The House of Lords thought differently and substituted a 50/50 apportionment. They
agreed that it was clearly not the job of the employer
to instruct a skilled man in the "technique of his craft"
but said that employers had a duty to instruct the
employee in and to enforce the employee's statutory obligations—at least those that were not serious.

This case is obviously important not merely for its severe
dilution of the sole-cause concept but also for the completely
new proposition that employers have an obligation to instruct
employees in their duties under the law. It cannot be forecast
yet how far this new principle will be taken, but it is clear
that it could have important effects not merely on the defence
of sole cause but on employers' liability as a whole. For the
present it is sufficient to say that the defence of sole cause
now appears to be limited to cases where there has been disobedience to a clear instruction on the part of a skilled employee.

(iii) *Hypothetical causes*

In the case of *Cummings* v. *Sir William Arrol & Co. Ltd.*
(1962) HL:

The plaintiff was a steel erector and was killed by a fall
from a high steel tower. The Building Regulations
required the employers to provide safety belts for "*such
persons who elect to use them*". No belts had been pro-

vided on the site and, of course, the erector had not been wearing one when he fell. There could be no doubt that the employers were in breach of statutory duty by their failure to provide safety belts but all the evidence indicated that if they had done so the dead man would not have used one. The House of Lords were unanimously of the opinion that the dead man's widow could recover nothing. The reasoning of the court was as follows: there were four steps in the causation of the accident, (i) a duty to supply a safety belt, (ii) a breach of that duty, (iii) that if there had been a safety belt the dead man would have used it, and (iv) that if there had been a safety belt the dead man would not have been killed. As all the evidence was that the dead man would *not* have used a belt had it been available, then the chain of causation is broken.

The decision in this case is not as startling as, perhaps, it seems at first sight. It is distinguishable from other statutory cases in that the dead man had a (very unusual) right of election under the regulations. Also it is difficult to see how it could be extended beyond this rather special class of breach of statutory duty.

(iv) *Remoteness*

The defence of remoteness means that the employer, whilst admitting responsibility for the act or omission that started a sequence, claims that the point at which the employee was injured is too far removed either in concept or in nature to be held to be the result of the act or omission. The example of the father committing suicide as a result of the death of his son at work is typical of an extreme remoteness problem. In one sense the son's death, which was the fault of the common employer, was the "cause" of the suicide. In another the two incidents can be regarded as totally non-related. The problems of remoteness are concerned with when the relationship can be regarded as broken.

Before 1961 there were few problems of remoteness in employers' liability. In *Re Polemis & Furness, Withy & Co.*

(1921) CA, the Court of Appeal had laid down the eminently
sensible rule that anything that happened as part of a direct
physical sequence, however unexpected, was not too remote
to be actionable. Liability in negligence could be regarded as
pushing over a line of dominoes. The person pushing over
the first one was responsible for the collapse of the last, however long the line and no matter how many blind corners it
turned. As claims under employers' liability are, by definition,
nearly always based on the direct physical consequences of
allegedly tortious acts, this meant that problems of remoteness
were few. In particular the "thin skull" cases, which in this
context are of obvious importance, created no problems. If
a man was negligently injured and the injury was exacerbated
because of the employee's physical peculiarity, liability was
undoubted.

Unfortunately the position was complicated by the decision
of the Judicial Committee of the Privy Council in *Overseas
Tankship (U.K.) Ltd.* v. *Morts Dock & Engineering Co. Ltd.*
(1961) PC known, for short, as *The Wagon Mound.* Here the
Court disapproved of the decision in *Re Polemis* and held that
the results of an action would be too remote if they were not
foreseeable. In other words, the end of the line of dominoes
has to be in contemplation before the fall of the last one can
give a right of action. Obviously this decision could have made
a great deal of difference to many cases in employers' liability.
The "thin skull" cases might have had to be re-thought. In
fact the application of *The Wagon Mound* does not appear
to have made a great deal of difference. In *Hughes* v. *Lord
Advocate* (1963) HL, the House of Lords held that burns from
a lamp left at a street excavation were foreseeable even though
the explosion of the lamp which caused the burns was not.
In *Smith* v. *Leech Brain & Co. Ltd.* (1962) QBD, Lord
Parker, C.J., held that cancer following a burn on a lip that
was already disposed to cancer was not too remote. Again
in *Warren* v. *Scruttons Ltd.* (1962), the unlikely result of
damage to the eyes following injury to a finger was held not
to be too remote.

It appears, therefore, that although *The Wagon Mound* may
have changed the law in general, its effect in the field of

employers' liability will be very slight if any. It is probably safest to assume that there will be liability in respect of almost any direct physical result of a tortious act, however unlikely.

There is one other aspect to the defence of remoteness: *novus actus interveniens*—the intervention of a new and independent cause that could not have been foreseen. ". . . something that I will call . . . extrinsic" (Lord Wright).

In the case of employers' liability it would appear that the only *novus actus* likely is a deliberate supervening human act. This may well be the true importance of disobedience to orders and it is probably safest to assume that only a deliberate disobedience to orders on the part of the plaintiff can be considered as a *novus actus*. Any other human act must be treated with great care before assuming that it can be a *novus actus* rather than contributory negligence. And the distinction is a very important one as a *novus actus* breaks the chain of causation and relieves the employer of *all* liability, whilst contributory negligence may relieve him only of part.

So, a doctor who took a grave risk to save life (*Baker v. T. E. Hopkins & Son* (1959) CA, employees who took risks to protect their employers' property (*Hyett v. Great Western Rail Co.* (1948)) CA and a deliberate act done by an employee without full realisation of the risk he ran (*Philco Radio & Television Corporation of Great Britain Ltd. v. J. Spurling Ltd.* (1949) CA have all been held not to constitute a *novus actus*. In *Pigney v. Pointer's Transport Services Ltd.* (1957) Norwich Assizes, even suicide was not enough when it resulted from a disturbed mental state due to injury to the head. Though in *Cowan v. National Coal Board* (1958) SC suicide *was* held to be a *novus actus* when it resulted from brooding on injuries and was not physically related to the original accident.

Insurance

The Employers' Liability (Compulsory Insurance Act) 1969 requires every employer (save nationalised industries and local authorities) to insure against employers' liability. The minimum cover is £2 million for each occurrence. In a recent case in the Court of Appeal (*Nettleship v. Weston* (1971) CA) a learner-driver who had an accident was held to be negligent although she had behaved in just the way a learner might be expected to. The court held that there was no such thing as a "reasonable learner-driver" (as opposed to an experienced one). They would demand the same skill and care irrespective of experience. The reason, said Lord Denning, was that all drivers are insured and thus able to bear loss. Therefore the courts will see that they are liable.

Now that the employer also has to have insurance, the courts could well apply the same principles to him (there were indications of such ideas in *Herrington's* case: see p. 137). If this line of thinking is pursued it will clearly strengthen the thesis of *noxa ipsa loquitur* propounded at p. 143 *et seq.*

Tailpiece

Since this chapter was written the House of Lords have decided the potentially important case of *Westwood* v. *The Post Office* (1973) HL:

> W. was employed by the Post Office in a three-storied building with a flat roof. With the Post Office's knowledge the employees used the roof during break-times. Access to the roof was by a staircase, by the top of which was a lift motor-room. On its door was a notice: "Only the authorised attendant is permitted to enter." W. went into the room, fell through the floor and was killed. At the trial the widow succeeded in an action for breach of statutory duty. The Court of Appeal reversed the decision. The House of Lords held that the Post Office *was* liable and W. was only 20% to blame.

The importance of this case is its contrast to *Uddin* (p. 150). Its similarities are obvious and, indeed, the House of Lords said that they were applying the same principles. But clearly they were not. The majority of the judges made it clear that they were concerned far more with the "causative potency" of the parties' acts and omissions than with their blameworthiness. If this was the case then the basis of assessment of contributory negligence suggested on pp. 150–151 may have to be radically modified in favour of the employee.

Chapter 10

Safety Legislation

I INTRODUCTION

At the time of writing workers in this country have the safety and health of their working environment controlled by ten major Acts of Parliament and nine more "of narrower scope". This mass of complex legislation is administered through seven different Government Departments and executed by several different bodies of inspectors. In addition, there is much subordinate legislation.

Despite this mass of law, more and more workers seem to be injured at work. It seems likely that about 1,000 are killed and 600,000 injured each year and some 23,000,000 working days lost. The problem is huge and the answer seems not to have been discovered. Concern with this situation led to the appointment of a committee under the chairmanship of Lord Robens with wide terms of reference which allowed them to look at the whole field of accident prevention at work. The committee reported in 1972 (Cmnd. 5034) and made radical and far-reaching recommendations. These can be summarised, very briefly, as follows:

1   The existing system is too complicated, too diffuse and has too much law in it. The committee recommended the establishment of a new National Authority for Safety and Health at Work embracing nearly all the existing statutory authorities.

2   The new authority should aim at promoting a more
    "self-regulating" system through the joint efforts of
    employers and workers.
3   Penal sanctions, such as fines, should be used only
    as a last resort when it is wished to make an example:
    the level of such sanctions should, therefore, be
    greatly increased.
4   The formal, precise, detailed regulation contained
    in existing statutes should be gradually replaced by
    flexible "voluntary" codes of practice, which would
    indicate acceptable standards and methods of achiev-
    ing them.
5   A new range of sanctions should be made available
    to inspectors, more in keeping with the recommended
    shift from a "police" to an "advisory" role. In par-
    ticular, the committee set great store by "Improve-
    ment Notices" specifying work to be done and condi-
    tional "Prohibition Notices" prohibiting the use of a
    machine, process or building until work had been
    done, with the technical merits of such notices being
    considered separately from the legal consequences of
    disobedience.
6   At the workplace itself each employer should be
    required to make a written statement of safety policy
    which would be made available to every employee.
    The employer would also be required to consult with
    his employees on safety matters.
7   The new legislation should apply to *all* employees.

In June 1973, the Government published a Consultative
Document setting out its proposals for the implementation of
the Robens Report. Broadly, the recommendations of the committee were accepted. But there were small but significant
changes of emphasis. While an advisory role for a new unified
safety administration was fully accepted, there was to be no
diminution of the "police" role and no great emphasis on self-
regulation. The advantage of codes of practice was seen
mainly to be their flexibility and ease of promulgation, especially in technical matters, rather than their voluntary nature.

In fact the document specifically states that the Government does not believe that the Robens Committee ever recommended a reduction in the amount of statutory protection in favour of a more voluntary system.

The main proposals of the Consultative Document are:

(i) That the administration of all safety legislation except that affecting agriculture should be unified under an independent Commission consisting of a Chairman and nine members (three appointed by the CBI, three by the TUC and three independent). The Commission will supervise the Executive and appoint its Director—and thus provide a buffer between the Minister and the Executive, which will have day-to-day responsibility.

(ii) A new Act will be passed covering all employed persons. This Act will have virtually no substance at all. It will, however, impose a new set of "basic obligations" upon employers, occupiers of premises, employees, manufacturers of plant and the self-employed. These basic obligations are additional and are, though wide, essentially negligence-based. They will be relevant only in criminal or enforcement proceedings and *not* in civil actions for breach of statutory duty. Their function seems likely to be a sort of general "safety net" to cover cases which do not fall precisely into some more detailed regulation.

(iii) The real substantive law—including, to begin with, everything that is found in the present Acts of Parliament and Codes of Regulations—will be found in new regulations. The first general task of the new authorities will be to re-write the huge mass of complicated law in a general, more rational way. It could take a long time. In addition to regulations, the Commission will have power to approve Codes of Practice. These will tend to be on technically complicated matters and will supplement the regulations. They have distinct legal significance.

(iv) The maximum penalties are to be greatly increased, including the possibility of unlimited fines with the "resources of the offender" being taken into account, and a general power to "order compliance" which could lead to imprisonment for contempt in case of disobedience. The Government have also accepted the idea of Improvement Notices and Prohibition Notices. These may be appealed against, on the technical aspects only, to the Industrial Tribunals, with special expert assessors, within a very short time period. Otherwise they must be complied with on pain of punishment, no defences based upon the merits of the action required in the notice being allowed at this stage. It is at this point that Codes of Practice, and the Basic Obligations, become relevant, for the Improvement and Prohibition Notices may be based on those as well as on the regulations.

At the time of writing, it is expected that legislation will shortly be presented to Parliament to start the inevitably long process outlined in the Robens Report and the Consultative Document. Nevertheless, it can be expected that the substance of the Factories Act 1961, the Offices, Shops and Railway Premises Act 1963 and the other legislation to be described in this chapter will remain with us in some form for several years to come. It is even fairly certain that the distinctions between the ambits of the various Acts (what is a "factory", etc.) will not disappear overnight.

The most important of the existing statutes, by sheer weight of the numbers of workers affected, are the Factories Act 1961 and the Offices, Shops and Railway Premises Act 1963. The Mines and Quarries Act 1954 has its own special importance in view of the particular hazards attached to the industry, but the specialist nature of legislation severely reduces its general interest save by way of consideration of its significant differences in method. The Agriculture (Safety, Health and Welfare) Act 1954 is the Cinderella of these major Acts because of difficulties of enforcement. The other Acts are of much less general importance.

All these Acts aim to control the safety, health and welfare of the work environment. Their ambits are defined by a mixture of place and activity. So a factory must have "premises" and persons must be "employed" in those premises in "factory process" (see p. 166). As explained earlier, many sections of these Acts give an individual the right to an action for breach of statutory duty if he is physically injured because of non-compliance. All operate on the basis of penalties for non-compliance with inspectorates having wide powers to enforce them.

Liability under this type of legislation is not usually put on the "employer" as such. The Factories Act and the Offices, Shops and Railway Premises Act put the responsibility for compliance on the "occupier" (see p. 166), the Mines and Quarries Act on the "owner". These persons are usually the employer as well but they need not be. Only in the Agricultural (Safety, Health and Welfare) Act is the "employer" responsible for implementation.

There are important differences between the requirements of these protective statutes and the demands of common law negligence. Some indication of these differences was given at p. 131 insofar as they affected the action for breach of statutory duty. In a criminal context there are many additional factors. So, whilst, as pointed out earlier, foreseeability (but see p. 180 for certain aspects of this), cost and inconvenience of remedy may be irrelevant to civil liability under this type of legislation, lack of knowledge of the breach, contributory negligence and the other "causal" defences are not available as a defence to a criminal prosecution here. After all, liability is not dependent, as it was in negligence cases, on the pre-existence of injury. Save for certain special cases involving elaborate third-party procedures which will be dealt with later, a breach of the requirements of the Act is all that needs to be proved to establish criminal liability on the part of the "occupier" or the "owner" or, in the case of agriculture, the "employer".

It follows, therefore, that criminal liability under this legislation is wider in scope than civil liability for breach of statutory duty. The occupier of a factory can be, and often is, liable to a fine for non-compliance when he is not liable to pay damages for injury caused by that non-compliance.

All these Acts are long and detailed. The object of this book is explanatory rather than expository. Consequently the sections that follow should be read in conjunction with the Acts themselves and regarded not as a substitute for them but as an aid to their understanding.

II THE FACTORIES ACT 1961: APPLICATION OF THE ACT

(i) A Factory

The definition section of the Act (s. 175) is vast. So is the judicial gloss. This is, perhaps inevitable in a section which attempts to deal with everything, but in general the refinements of borderline cases, though amusing if you have time, can be ignored. For all practical purposes a factory is:

(*a*) premises where
(*b*) persons are employed
(*c*) in manual labour
(*d*) by way of trade or for the purposes of gain
(*e*) in a "factory process".

All this is subject to an overriding judicial interpretation that, in cases of doubt, the general purpose of the establishment shall be looked at. And that this general purpose shall be industrial or, at least, quasi-industrial.

> The plaintiff was employed in a chemist's shop doing work which clearly came within the scope of the definition. The other five persons working in the shop were not employed in manual labour. The judge held that the plaintiff's manual labour was only incidental to the purposes of the shop which were to be a retail chemist's shop. The premises were, therefore, not a factory.
>
> *Joyce* v. *Boots Cash Chemists (Southern) Ltd.* (1950) QBD

Each of these five criteria needs individual explanation.

(*a*) *Premises*

Buildings are not necessary, but there must be some clearly definable area; though there need be no walls or fences. Woodworking machinery used in a forest does not make the forest a factory even though the other four criteria are satisfied.

There is no sufficiently definable area. Where a building is occupied as a factory with adjoining land serving it, the whole area is a factory and not just the building. Equally, part of a building may be a factory whilst the rest is not.

(b) *Employed*

Before premises can be a factory someone must be employed in them in the master–servant relationship. If six partners work together in a machine shop, that shop is not a factory. If they decide to employ one boy to sweep the floor or make the tea it is enough to change the shop into a factory. Equally, if the six decide to form themselves into a limited liability company the premises become a factory for the six former partners now become the employees of the company.

For this reason alone prisons, technical colleges and universities are not factories even though they produce articles which are, at times, sold.

(c) *Manual labour*

The term is used in contradistinction to purely intellectual activity. It is not restricted to sweat-causing, muscle-cracking work.

> "One has to look in each case at the exercise of the employment of the person under consideration, and ascertain whether the work that he is employed to do is primarily manipulative rather than intellectual or artistic" (Lord Parker, C.J., in *Haygarth* v. *J. & F. Stone* (1963) DC).

(d) *By way of trade or for purposes of gain*

The "or" is disjunctive. If there is a trade there is no need to consider gain. Similarly the disjunctive nature of the "or" dissociates the word "gain" completely from the word "trade". In other words the "gain" need not be direct (as opposed to indirect).

> A consulting engineer specialised in the testing of materials. He employed persons in manual labour to work a laboratory concrete mixer and crushing machine to test

materials physically prior to making his reports. He received fees for his reports. The premises used for these tests was held to be a factory.

Hendon Corporation v. *Stanger* (1948) CA

Section 175(9) provides that premises in the occupation of the Crown or any other public authority do not escape being a factory simply because they are not operated by way of trade or for purposes of gain if the other criteria are satisfied.

(e) *In a "factory process"*

There is no legal justification for the term "factory process" but, like "employers' liability", it is a useful term to describe a rather complicated situation. It is probably accurate to say that if something is done to "an article" which alters its condition in any way then it is a "factory process". Thus manufacturing, cleaning or repairing "an article" are all "factory processes". So is "breaking bulk". Sorting is not a "factory process" as nothing is done to the article.

The word "article" has a very wide meaning. Water is "an article" and, therefore, premises used for filtering water are a factory. Premises where water is merely pumped are not. A live animal is not "an article" nor is an electrical impulse.

(ii) **The Occupier**

The obligations under the Act are placed on the "occupier" save for a few relatively unimportant cases where the owners of a building in multiple occupation have duties in respect of facilities used in common (ss. 120–122).

It is noteworthy that whilst wide obligations are put on the employee in respect of *his own* compliance with the Act (see p. 174) none are put on him in respect of compliance with the Act in general. A Bill was before Parliament prior to the General Election of 1970 which would have given workers collectively certain positive rights and duties under the Act, but, like all Bills at this stage, it failed to survive the election.

The term "occupier" is not defined and this lack of definition has proved beneficial. In general the "occupier" is the person with control over the factory and "control" here means ultimate financial and therefore physical control. Usually there are no problems. Most factories are run by limited companies and the company is the "occupier".

The control concept means that an occupier can rid himself from liability for part of his factory by relinquishing "control" of it. There seems to be no reason why in, say, the case where contractors are in the factory the occupier should not formally hand over control of any part which can be physically defined to them, thus divesting himself of all responsibility under the Act for what goes on in that part. The handing over of control would, of course, have to be actual and not merely theoretical.

(iii) **Persons Covered by the Act**

As explained earlier (see p. 133) not everyone in the premises is entitled to the protection of the Act. Whilst it is possible that the case of *Hartley* v. *Mayoh* was wrongly decided on the facts it is unlikely that the principles upon which that case was decided will be changed. To have the benefit of the Act, a person must be working in the factory on matters directly connected with the work of the factory. When the connection becomes "indirect" is hard to say, but it appears that factory inspectors, policemen and representatives calling on the factory do not come into this category. Though they will, of course, have the benefit of the Occupiers' Liability Act (see p. 136).

(iv) **Enforcement**

The Act is enforced by the Factory Inspectorate of the Department of Employment. In addition to the Chief Inspector and Deputy Chief Inspectors, the day-to-day running of the Inspectorate depends on 11 Divisions each headed by a Superintending Inspector. The Divisions are sub-divided into semi-autonomous Districts each in the charge of a District Inspector. The name of the Superintending Inspector and that of the Inspector for the District must be displayed on the abstract of the Act (Form 1) that is posted in every factory.

Only the Chief Inspector and the District Inspector are mentioned in the Act. Both have certain powers of certification and approval. For instance, the Chief Inspector may grant exemption by certificate from certain of the provisions of s. 31 regarding precautions with respect to explosive or inflammable dust, gas, vapour or other substances. The District Inspector may allow freedom from posting a notice under s. 2 specifying the numbers of persons who may work in any workroom.

The job of the Superintending Inspector, as his title implies, is to oversee the operation of the districts in his division and to act as a link with the Chief Inspector. One of his more important functions is the approval of prosecutions.

Inspectors have wide powers which are, in general, used with discretion. The most important are:

1   The right of entry to a *known* factory at any time of the day or night when the inspector has reasonable cause to believe that anyone is employed in the factory. The inspector need make no reference to the occupier or his agents before, or at the time of, entering (s. 146(1) (*a*)).

2   The right to take a policeman with him if he has reasonable cause to fear obstruction (s. 146(1) (*b*)).

   Any person who obstructs an inspector is liable to a fine of £20. If the obstruction takes place in a factory the occupier is also guilty of an offence (s. 146(4)).

3   The right of entry *by day only* (on the same terms as above) into any premises that the inspector has reasonable cause to believe to be a factory (s. 146(1) (*a*)).

4   The right to examine all registers, certificates, notices, etc., kept in pursuance of the Act and to make such copies as he sees fit (s. 146(1) (*c*)).

5   The right to inspect the premises to see whether the Act is being complied with (s. 146(1) (*a*)).

6   The right to examine any person working in the factory (or who has worked in it during the previous

two months) about any matter relating to the Act in the factory. The inspector may also require such persons to make and sign a statutory declaration (s. 146(1) (*f*)).

It is important to note that the inspector has the right to question such persons *alone*. Neither employer nor trade union representative has the right to be present if the inspector decides that they shall not be. Even a solicitor has no right to be there.

7   The power to take samples of any material used in a factory which, in the inspector's opinion, is likely to cause bodily injury to persons employed (s. 78). "In his opinion" presumably means what it says. The inspector will not have to justify the opinion so long as he held it at the time the sample was taken.

8   The right to conduct proceedings in a magistrates' court in prosecutions under the Act (s. 149).

An inspector has *no* power to stop, or in any other way interfere with, the working of any machine, plant or process. This does not prevent them from doing so in extreme cases, but it is an excess of their powers. (But see p. 171.)

A substantial proportion of the Act is designed to assist the inspector in the exercise of his powers.

III   NOTIFICATION OF ACCIDENTS, DOCUMENTATION, ETC.

Section 80 requires the occupier to notify the district inspector on the prescribed form (Form 43) of any accident which causes death to a person employed in the factory or keeps such a person from earning full wages at his normal work for more than three days. The occupier must also notify any accidents to persons in the factory not in his employment. The precise nature of the obligation is important. Notification depends *not* on whether the injured person is at work or not, but on whether he can earn full wages *at his normal work*.

Section 81 requires similar notification of "dangerous

occurrences" whether or not they have caused injury. They are defined in the Dangerous Occurrences (Notification) Regulations 1947 and include such potentially lethal events as the collapse of a crane, the bursting of a grinding wheel, etc.

Section 82 requires the notification of certain industrial diseases.

It will be seen that this system of notification is a form of self-inspection. It is not known how effective it is. The temptation not to notify an accident that might lead to legal proceedings is very strong. A limited amount of cross-checking is possible because of the requirement that reportable accidents be entered in the General Register (*q.v.* below). But this is not very reliable either.

The process of self-inspection by the occupier is continued by the documentation required by the Act. Before the factory goes into operation the occupier has to notify the district inspector (s. 137). There is, however, no obligation to wait for permission to start operations. Notification is all that is required. Every factory must also keep certain documents available for inspection. The General Register (Form 31) is, perhaps, the most important and s. 140 lays down various particulars that must be entered in it. Also, by s. 166, any entry made in the General Register is evidence of the facts stated in that entry. Conversely any failure to make an entry is evidence that the requirements relating to that entry have not been carried out. In addition, many of the sections relating to plant and equipment require certificates of test to be available for inspection at all times. For example, s. 36 requires that each air receiver shall have a test certificate which must be attached to the General Register. There are similar provisions for hoists and lifts (s. 22), lifting tackle (s. 26) and cranes (s. 27).

Section 138 requires the display of the official summary of the Act (Form 1). There are similar requirements for abstracts of all codes of regulations to which the factory is subject. These are all badly written and poorly produced documents which are seldom read. They are intended to draw the attention of persons employed to their rights and duties under the Act and regulations.

The inspectorate has, in recent years, regarded its functions as primarily advisory. Prosecution is always a last resort. (In 1972 only 1,547 firms were prosecuted.) To assist them as advisers the inspectorate has an intelligence section and various specialist departments in addition to the "routine" inspectorate. The services of these sections are always available free of charge to occupiers who wish to use them.

Finally, it should be said that, through no fault of its own, the inspectorate cannot possibly do its job properly. There are approximately 600 inspectors engaged upon day-to-day routine inspection. Some 200,599 premises were registered under the Act in 1972, 258,137 accidents were reported, and 296,210 official visits were made. Simple arithmetic shows that adequate, efficient inspection is impossible.

IV PENALTIES

An occupier who fails to carry out any requirement of the Act is guilty of an offence. Some sections specify the penalty for non-compliance. For instance, s. 159 provides for a fine of £100 or imprisonment for three months for falsification of certain documents.

Where the section does not stipulate its own penalty the occupier is liable to a fine not exceeding £60 or, where the contravention was likely to cause death or bodily injury, to a fine not exceeding £300.

Clearly such maxima are ridiculously low and the magistrates' courts do not help. In 1972 the average fine in prosecutions based on safety provisions was £52. No figures are available for health, welfare and employment prosecutions, but the average for the latter two in 1971 was £11. It is fortunate that most occupiers have an instinctive dislike of being prosecuted which is not based on the size of the probable penalty.

In addition to the financial penalties described above there are two more very important, though little used, penal sections of the Act.

Section 54 gives power to a magistrates' court (including a single magistrate sitting alone) to make an order, on complaint by an inspector, forbidding a process or the use of any machine or plant in a factory. This order can be made *ex parte* (that is without the other side being heard) when there is "imminent risk of serious bodily injury" to someone employed. Though, where an *ex parte* order is granted a full hearing must be arranged at the "earliest opportunity".

Any order made under this section may be absolute and permanent or temporary. The order may require work, such as repairs, to be done.

Section 55 gives a *full* magistrates' court (*i.e.* a stipendiary magistrate sitting alone or not less than two lay-justices) similar powers in respect of the actual factory *building*. In this case the order can *not* be made *ex parte*.

The potential importance of these two sections cannot be overstressed. Especially in the light of the limitations on the inspectors' powers mentioned at (iv) above. It is unfortunate that they are so little used. There were only 33 such applications in 1972.

It would appear that any person can institute proceedings under the Act save that ss. 54 and 55 depend on complaint by an inspector. So far as the authors are aware no private person, trade union or employer has ever made use of their right to institute proceedings.

Obviously, the fact that the occupier can be liable under the Act when he did not know of the breach, and had, perhaps, made great efforts to prevent it, could be unfair. For that reason s. 161 provides for a special procedure whereby the occupier can absolve himself in certain cases. If he is charged with an offence and he can show that he has used "all due diligence" to enforce the Act and that the offence has been committed without his "consent connivance or wilful default" then he has two courses open to him.

First, if he knows who was responsbile for the breach of the Act he can cross-summons that person. The occupier, the third party and the prosecution then all go to court together. The prosecution first proves that an offence was committed and the other parties fight it out as to who was responsible for it. If it is held to be the third party then he is guilty *of the offence with which the occupier was originally charged.* Not, that is, with an offence under s. 143 (q.v. below). For that matter, the third party might well not be employed in the factory.

If the occupier does not know who the third party is, a second course is open to him. If he can show that he used "all due diligence" and produce evidence that someone else must have been responsible for the breach even though he cannot be identified, this is a good defence.

> A dangerous part of machinery (see p. 180) was fenced by surrounding the whole machine by a fence 4' high entered by a gate. The gate was controlled by a key which also fitted into the electrical control panel for the machine. Thus, in theory, the key must be taken out of the panel cutting off the electricity to the machine before the gate could be opened. The key could not be taken out of the panel without switching off the power. Nor could it be taken out of the gate until it has been locked shut. An employee wanted to do some work on the machine. He found the gate was open and assumed that the power was off. While he was working on the machine it moved and he was injured. The company were prosecuted for breach of s. 14(1) of the Act.
>
> On investigation it was shown that some person unknown (but assumed to be an employee of the company) had forced the lock thus destroying the safety procedure. At the magistrates' court four points were established: (i) the machine was inspected "every two or three days" and supervisory staff were instructed to report any defects; (ii) the company employed safety officers; (iii) the gate would need to be opened only to carry out maintenance; (iv) the company did not know that the lock had been forced.
>
> The magistrates dismissed the charge and the Divisional Court upheld them.

Wright v. *Ford Motor Co. Ltd.* (1966) DC

It is by no means clear what "all due diligence" means. Presumably *Wright's* case above gives a fair idea of the sort of precautions that the courts will accept: doing all that you can reasonably be expected to do in a given set of circumstances.

V   DUTIES OF EMPLOYED PERSONS UNDER THE FACTORIES ACT

No obligations are placed on employed persons either as individuals or collectively for the implementation of the Act as a whole. Nevertheless s. 143 places wide duties on the individual in respect of his personal behaviour.

Section 143(1) provides that where the occupier has provided anything *because of an obligation placed on him by the Act* the employee must use it if it is for his health or safety and not interfere with it or abuse it if it is for his welfare. So, if a guard is provided for a dangerous part of machinery as required by s. 14(1), the employee must use it. If towels are provided as part of the washing facilities under s. 58, the employee is committing an offence if he cleans his shoes on them.

Section 143(2) is even wider in its scope:

> "No person employed in a factory . . . shall wilfully and without reasonable cause do anything likely to endanger himself or others."

There is no equivalent "omnibus" clause placing a similar responsibility on the occupier. "Wilfully" in this context only means "of his own free will" as opposed to under duress or orders; though it excludes carelessness where there is real inadvertence. Obviously the scope is very wide indeed and the subsection covers anything from punching a fellow-workman on the nose to riding a motor-bike too fast round the factory roads.

> A labourer in an oil-blending factory persuaded some youths of 15 and 16 to join with him in filling 1 lb. oil tins with naphthalene. They hammered the lids on tight and threw them into the firebox of the steam boiler in the factory so that they could enjoy the explosions. One

tin did not explode so the labourer opened the firebox door to see what had happened to it. The tin exploded as he opened the door and he and three of the youths were burned. The stipendiary magistrate convicted the man of a breach of s. 143(2) and he was fined.

The maximum penalty under the section is £15, but where the contravention was "likely to cause the death of, or bodily injury to, any person" the maximum is increased to £75.

It is not clear from the Act what the maximum penalty for an employed person is when he is convicted under the third-party procedures outlined above. As he is convicted of the occupier's offence and not of an offence under s. 143, it is at least arguable that he is liable to the occupier's maximum penalty of £300. Not that any court would award such a penalty.

VI THE SUBSTANTIVE PROVISIONS OF THE FACTORIES ACT

The Act has two main objects: to regulate the employment of certain protected classes of persons and to control the health, safety and welfare of the working environment. The effect of the restrictions on hours of work was discussed in Chapter 2. All that is necessary to say here is that the hours of work of women and young persons (between 16 and 18) are elaborately controlled and that children below the age of 16 are prohibited from working in a factory.

Many of the provisions controlling the work-environment need no comment. Some sections are nothing but lists of things that must, or must not, be done. There is no difficulty in understanding them. For instance, s. 34 lays down elaborate provisions in respect of the maintenance, examination and use of steam boilers. The section is long and tedious to read, but there are no problems of interpretation: there is no "law" to be discussed in the section.

One exception to this general dismissal of so much of the Act is the use, in a number of sections otherwise consisting purely of "shopping-lists", of such stock phrases as "reasonably practicable" (*e.g.* s. 22(6)), "properly maintained" (s. 22(1)). A short glossary of the most common of such terms is, therefore, worth while:

(*a*) *"Good mechanical construction, sound material and adequate strength"; "sound construction"*

These, in more or less any combination, mean much the same thing: that the thing to which they refer shall be suitable in construction, material and strength *to do the job it is intended to do*. It is a *continuing* obligation: not only must the thing comply when it is first put into use: it must be kept that way. The standard is *not* absolute. The mere fact that something breaks when in use does *not* necessarily mean that there is a breach of the requirement. It may have been used for some purpose for which it was never intended.

(*b*) *"Properly maintained" or "maintained"*

These words *do* create an absolute standard. "Maintained" is defined in s. 176(1) as "maintained in an efficient state, in efficient working order, and in good repair". If this standard is not kept up then the reason or lack of it is irrelevant: there is a breach of the requirement.

(*c*) *"Reasonably practicable" or "practicable"*

These words are very difficult to construe. There is an ascending order of liability depending on the precise phrase used. "Reasonably practicable" is a lower standard than "practicable", which is, in its turn, of course, a lower standard than "physically possible".

Unfortunately it is not possible to define "practicability" with any precision. The best you can say is that "reasonably practicable" is analogous to "foreseeability" in common law negligence as described in Chapter 9. The criteria, as there, appear to be the state of knowledge and the balancing of cost against risk. If the word "practicable" is used without qualification the risk weighs a little more heavily against the cost.

It is up to the defence to show that something was not "practicable" or "reasonably practicable".

(d) *"Prevent"*

The use of this word without qualification is the ultimate in absoluteness. If the section requires that the occupier "prevent" something happening then, if it does happen, there is a breach without any further argument.

(e) *"Prescribed"*

This means prescribed by the Minister, *i.e.* the Secretary for Employment and Productivity.

The Fencing of Machinery

For obvious reasons, the provisions contained in ss. 12–21 have been the subject of most judicial consideration. The law on these sections has, therefore, inevitably become complex and needs special consideration.

(a) *The meaning of "machinery"*

"Machinery" is not defined in the Act. It includes machinery that is not moved by mechanical power. A foot- or hand-operated guillotine is just as much a "machine" as a power-driven one.

The judicial interpretation of the word has been restrictive. Machinery is only machinery for the purposes of the Act when it is fully installed as part of the factory equipment and is used or intended to be used in, or ancillary to, the factory processes:

> One sack-hoist of seven to be installed in a mill had been completed. It had not been taken into commercial use as the whole installation of which the sack-hoist was to form a part was not complete. It was held that, as the sack-hoist itself was complete and was destined for use as process machinery in the mill it was "machinery" within the meaning of the Act.

Irwin v. *White, Tomkins & Courage Ltd.* (1964) HL

A machine manufactured for sale in the factory is not "machinery" within the meaning of the Act.

Parvin v. *Morton Machine Co. Ltd.* (1952) HL

Similarly, a machine under repair in a factory is not "machinery" unless it is part of the factory's own installation.

Thorogood v. *Van den Berghs & Jergens Ltd.* (1951) CA

This approach has some odd, illogical results. A manufacturer of machines is, presumably, allowed to make his machines, to run them and to test them prior to sale without any guarding at all. Should he, however, decide to keep one of his own products to help to make further machines, the moment he takes that decision, that machine becomes subject to the Act. It is easy to imagine circumstances where two identical machines are operating side by side, one subject to the Act and the other not.

(b) Classes of "machinery"

The Act divides "machinery" into three classes: prime movers, transmission machinery and "other dangerous parts of machinery". A prime mover is the source of the energy which drives the process machinery; it can be an electric motor, a steam engine, a waterwheel or a windmill. The term is defined in s. 176(1). Transmission machinery is the machinery which transmits the energy from the prime mover to the process machinery; it can be a shaft or a belt, a clutch or a train of gears. The huge residual group "other dangerous parts of machinery" refers to every machine (within the meaning of the Act) that is not a prime mover or transmission machinery.

Each of these three classes of machinery is treated slightly differently and the difference is important.

1. *Prime movers.* Section 12 provides that:

"Every flywheel directly connected to any prime mover and every moving part of any prime mover . . . shall be

securely fenced whether the prime mover is situated in
an engine house or not."

This means that every moving part of a prime mover has to
be "securely fenced" (see below for the meaning of this term)
irrespective of where it is. Even if the prime mover is locked
up in a room on its own the moving parts must be securely
fenced inside the locked door. The only exception to this rule
is that allowed by s. 12(3) which allows electric motors and
their flywheel and pulleys to rely on safety by position. This
exception is discussed in general below, but here it certainly
means that the electric motor enclosed behind the locked door
does not need to have its flywheel securely fenced. Nor does
the motor tucked away 50′ high in the roof.

   2. *Transmission machinery.*—Section 13 provides:

"Every part of the transmission machinery shall be
securely fenced unless it is in such a position or of such
construction as to be as safe to every person employed
or working on the premises as it would be if securely
fenced."

This is a less stringent standard than that set for prime
movers. You can run your line-shafting unfenced provided that
no one approaches it.

   3. *Other dangerous parts of machinery.*—Section 14(1)
provides:

"Every dangerous part of any machinery other than prime
movers and transmission machinery shall be securely
fenced unless it is in such a position or of such construction as to be as safe to every person employed or working
on the premises as it would be if securely fenced."

A new element has been introduced here: that of danger.
Transmission machinery and the moving parts of prime
movers are *assumed* to be dangerous. When dealing with the
residual class danger has to be *proved*. It should also be noted
that the section speaks of "parts of machinery" and *not* of
"machines".

   There are, therefore, three points to be considered: what

constitutes safety by position? what is meant by "dangerous"? and what is meant by "securely fenced"?

(c) Safety by position

Put simply, this depends on results. If someone is hurt on a part of machinery then it is impossible to argue that it was safe by position (though it can be argued that it was securely fenced: see below). The occupier relies on safety by position at his peril.

> A workman was instructed to move a belt from a shaft to a pulley while the shaft was revolving. The place was not accessible in the normal way and the man had to climb up a ladder and stand on a beam. It was held that the shaft was not safe by position.

> *Atkinson* v. *London & North-Eastern Rail Co.* (1926) CA

> Nor is it enough to say that a machine is safe "by construction" if the operator does as he is told. Safety "by construction" is also only justified by results.

> *Sutherland* v. *Exors. of James Mills Ltd.* (1928) DC

(d) "Dangerous"

A part of machinery is dangerous if it is ". . . a reasonably foreseeable cause of injury to anybody acting in a way in which a human being may be reasonably expected to act in circumstances which may be reasonably expected to occur." This is not the test of "reasonableness" described in Chapter 9 when negligence was discussed. The standard of reasonableness here is lower than that and covers ". . . the careless and inattentive worker whose inadvertent or indolent conduct may expose him to risk of injury or death from the unguarded part" (Lord Cooper in *Mitchell* v. *North British Rubber Co. Ltd.* (1945) SC).

What is more, the test is an abstract one. The court does not consider the facts in the case before it and decide whether what the injured person did was foreseeable. They consider the nature of the part of machinery and ask whether a *hypo-*

thetical person acting in a reasonably foreseeable way could be injured on the part of machinery. If they could then it is dangerous. This is often called the "dangling tie" test. The behaviour of the injured person prior to his injury may be relevant in a civil action as contributory negligence. It is irrelevant to the criminal responsibility of the occupier.

> A workman chased a pigeon from one workshop into another he had no right to be in. He wanted to kill the bird and eat it. He followed it up into the roof and was caught on the unfenced shaft. His employers were liable though they could not possibly have imagined such an unlikely set of circumstances.
>
> *Uddin* v. *Associated Portland Cement Manufacturers Ltd.* (1965) CA

When considering whether a part of machinery is dangerous or not the machine must be looked at as it will be in use. The actual working of the machine and the components in it must be considered.

> A workman was injured when feeding a metal bar into some straightening rollers. The bars were fed by presenting them by hand to "leading-in" rollers. In the absence of the bar the rollers were harmless because the gap between them was wider than a man's arm. It was held, however, that a trap between the rollers, the bar and the arm was a dangerous part of machinery.
>
> *Midland and Low Moor Iron & Steel Co. Ltd.* v. *Cross* (1965) HL

(e) "Securely fenced"

If a part of machinery is dangerous it must be "securely fenced". Secure fencing means a barricade that prevents contact with the part being fenced by (as in the case of "danger") by anyone acting in a reasonably foreseeable manner. There are, therefore, limits to what can be expected of the fencing: the obligation is not absolute.

A boy was cleaning cocoa beans off a shelf working from a ladder. He had propped his ladder against a revolving shaft. The ladder slipped and he fell. As he did so his hand went into some gears close to the shelf. The gears were guarded at the front but not at the back and sides. There was held not to have been a breach of s. 13 as an approach to the gears from this angle could not have been foreseen.

Burns v. *Joseph Terry & Sons Ltd.* (1951) CA.

Whilst the above case was almost certainly wrongly decided on the facts, the principle of applying foreseeability to the duty to fence as well as to the concept of danger is now well established.

Once there is a duty to fence then there is no escape from the duty. The part of machinery must be securely fenced even if it means that it cannot be used.

A man was injured on a small grinding wheel. As much of the wheel as could be if it were to be used had been enclosed. Only the small opening needed to use the wheel had been left open. It was held that this was not secure fencing because of the small gap. The fact that the machine could not be used if it were securely fenced was irrelevant.

John Summers & Sons Ltd v. *Frost* (1955) HL

The duty to fence is, however, only to fence against contact, there is no duty to protect against the machine throwing out either parts of itself or components.

An operator's eye was injured when a drill broke and he was struck by a particle of it. There was held to be no breach of s. 14.

Close v. *Steel Co. of Wales Ltd.* (1962) HL

(*f*) *"In motion or in use"*

If a part of machinery has to be fenced then s. 16 requires that the fence be kept in position whilst the machinery is "in motion or in use". These words have been interpreted by the courts not as meaning "moving or being used" but as something rather less.

A man was injured on the revolving rollers of a printing machine. There was no doubt that these rollers were a dangerous part of machinery. In order to clean the rollers the guard had been removed and they were being "inched" round very slowly under power. The Court of Appeal decided that the rollers were neither in motion nor in use.

Knight v. *Leamington Spa Courier Ltd.* (1961) CA

In another almost identical case upon a similar machine an inching button was not being used and the motor had to be switched on and off quickly. It was held that the rollers were in use.

Stanbrook v. *Waterlow & Sons Ltd.* (1964) CA

A fitter was examining the workings of a lathe. He wanted to move the collar of the machine a few inches. He could have done this by hand but did it by switching the machine on and off very quickly. In the course of his previous work he had removed the guard from some gearing and his fingers were trapped in the gears when he switched on. It was held that the lathe was not in motion nor in use.

Mitchell v. *W. S. Westin Ltd.* (1965) CA

Obviously with such a confusion of cases in the Court of Appeal, it is hard to lay down any hard and fast rule as to the law on this important practical point. It might well be, however, that the following criteria decide whether a machine is "in motion or in use":

(i) *The speed at which the machine is running.* If it is running at full speed it will always be "in motion". There comes a point, however, to which the speed is reduced when it will not be in motion. The exact point cannot be specified.

(ii) *The method of starting and stopping the machinery.* The machine is much less likely to be regarded as "in motion" if a proper inching device is being used.

(iii) *The duration of the movement.*

(iv) *The purpose of the movement* at least to the extent that the machine will always be regarded as "in use" if it is being used for the purpose for which it was installed (as opposed to cleaning, etc.).

(g) Removing guards in general

Obviously the discussion on "in motion or in use" indicates one set of circumstances when guards may legitimately be removed even though the machinery is "in motion" or "in use". There is one other.

Section 16 must be read in conjunction with s. 15: "Provisions as to unfenced machinery" and the Operations at Unfenced Machinery Regulations made under the section. (For a discussion of regulations and their significance in general see p. 119). The section allows work at unfenced machinery, provided the terms of the regulations are observed, in two cases:

(1) The examination of a part of machinery in motion when such an examination *can only be carried out with the guard removed and the machinery in motion.* And, following the examination, any lubrication or adjustment that the examination has shown to be necessary where the lubrication and adjustment *can only be carried out with the part of machinery in motion.*

This exemption is very often misunderstood. It should not be, for it means exactly what it says. "Can only be carried out" does *not* mean that doing it this way is quicker, easier, cheaper or a good deal less troublesome in general. It means that the work cannot be done in any other way. There are very few operations indeed which comply with these strict conditions. Nor does "lubrication or adjustment" include repair.

In addition to the strict terminology of s. 15, s. 16 with which it is linked allows the exemption only when the part of machinery is *"necessarily"* exposed for examination and subsequent lubrication and adjustment. Once again the term used implies that there is no alternative.

(2) The second state of affairs where work is allowed on unfenced machinery is quite different and is lessening in importance as line-shafting becomes less common. The mounting or shipping of belts and the lubrication of transmission machinery are allowed, provided the full requirements of the regulations are complied with, in certain processes which are listed in the regulations. They are all "continuous processes" where there would be grave inconvenience, or even danger, if they were stopped to allow work of this kind to be done.

In order to claim either of the two exemptions claimed above, the whole of the provisions of the Operations at Unfenced Machinery Regulations must be observed. The main requirements are:

(i) The work may be carried out only by male persons over the age of 18 who have been appointed *in writing* as "machinery attendants", have been sufficiently trained in the work and the dangers arising from it, issued with a special leaflet (Form 280) and had their names entered in the General Register (see p. 170).

(ii) Except in the case of a toolsetter "or other skilled mechanic" all such work must be done wearing a one-piece overall (provided by the occupier) with no external pockets or other projections, with another person within sight or hearing (commonly known as within "screaming distance"), and, if from a ladder, with the ladder securely lashed or held.

If any detail of these requirements, however, trivial, is not complied with then the occupier loses the right to claim the exemption (*Nash* v. *High Duty Alloys* (1947) CA).

It must be stressed, because of the wide misapprehensions in industry, that there are *no* further exemptions from the requirements of fencing other than those detailed above. There is *no* exemption for toolrooms; there is *no* exemption for fitters, wheelwrights or other skilled men. It will immediately

be seen that most machinery attendants have been appointed
to no purpose.

(*h*) *Women, young persons and machinery*

Women and young persons receive additional protection
under the Act.

Section 20 provides:

> "A woman or young person shall not clean any part of
> a prime mover or of any transmission machinery while
> the prime mover or transmission machinery is in motion,
> and shall not clean any part of any machine if the clean-
> ing thereof would expose the woman or young person
> to risk of injury from any moving part either of that
> machine or of any adjacent machinery."

Clearly, in some ways this section is tautological. The cleaning
of a prime mover or of transmission machinery in motion will
normally be in breach of s. 12 or s. 13 at any rate, though
the provision in respect of prime movers seems to go a little
further than s. 12. The prohibition seems to apply even if the
moving parts of the prime mover are securely fenced. Probably
"in motion" here means the same as it does in s. 16, but Winn,
J., refused to hold that it did in *Kelly* v. *John Dale Ltd.* (1965)
QBD, saying that he did not need to decide the point. He
then went on to say that "moving" did *not* mean the same
as "in motion" in s. 16 but meant precisely what it said.

Section 20 deals with both women and young persons. Section 21 is concerned with young persons only. It is also the
only section of the Act that deals with "dangerous machines"
as opposed to "dangerous parts of machinery".

The section provides that any young person working at a
machine classified by the Minister as "dangerous" under the
section must

    (i) be instructed in the dangers of the machine;
    (ii) have received sufficient training; *or*
    (iii) be under adequate supervision by a person who has
         a thorough knowledge of the machine.

Eighteen machines have so far been specified under the

Dangerous Machines (Training of Young Persons) Order 1954
(S.I. 1954 No. 921).

Non-Legal Interpolation

The problems of assessing which parts of machinery are
dangerous and which are not are well known to judges, lawyers, factory inspectors and all who work in industry. It is
all too rarely that one can say, like Browne, J. in *Leach* v.
Standard Telephones and Cables Ltd. (1966) QBD:

> "The first question is whether this circular saw blade,
> which revolved at about seven to eight hundred revolu-
> tions per minute, was a dangerous part of any
> machinery. It is enough to say it obviously was."

Instead, we are caught up in problems of foreseeability both
in terms of danger and of fencing. It is possible, however,
to approach most fencing problems in a manner similar to that
of Browne, J., and to come to the right conclusion most of
the time. It must be stressed that the suggestion that follows
has no legal standing whatsoever. It is, however, of great practical use and many, including the authors, believe that some
such approach could usefully be incorporated into future legislation.

In 1947, Mr. H. A. Hepburn, then Deputy Chief Inspector
of Factories, gave a paper to the Institution of Mechanical
Engineers on "The Fencing of Dangerous Parts of
Machinery". In the course of this paper he propounded certain
"axioms": that the following parts, or combination of parts,
of machinery are dangerous within the meaning of the Act.
The authors believe this to be an accurate statement of the
law.

(1) Revolving shafts, couplings, spindles, mandrels, and bars.
    (Line and countershafts; drill spindles and attach-
    ments; boring bars; stock bars; and the like.)
(2) In-running nips between pairs of revolving parts.
    (Gear wheels; friction wheels; calendar bowls; mangle
    rolls; metal manufacturing rolls; rubber breaking and
    mixing rolls and others.)

(3) In-running nips of the belt and pulley type.
   (Belts and pulleys, plain, flanged, or grooved; chain and sprocket gears; conveyor belts and pulleys; metal coiling; and the like.)

(4) Nips between connecting rods or links and rotating wheels, cranks, or disks.
   (Side motions of certain flat-bed printing machines; jacquard and other automatic looms; and various other machines.)

(5) Nips between reciprocating and fixed parts, other than tools and dies.
   (Metal planer reversing stops; sliding tables and fixtures; cotton spinning mule carriages and back stops, pillars, etc.; shaping machine tables and fixtures; tool steady guide and steady arm on turret lathe; and others.)

(6) Nips between revolving control handles and fixed parts.
   (Traverse gear handles of lathes, millers, and the like.)

(7) Nips between revolving wheels or cylinders, and pans or tables.
   (Sand mixers; edge runners; crushing and incorporating mills; dough brakes; mortar mills; leather currying machines; and others.)

(8) Projections on revolving parts.
   (Key-heads; set screws; cotter pins; coupling bolts; and the like.)

(9) Revolving open-arm pulleys and other discontinuous rotating parts.
   (Pulleys; fan blades; spur gearwheels; and the like.)

(10) Revolving beaters, spiked cylinders, and drums.
   (Scutchers; rag-flock teasers; cotton openers; laundry washers; and the like.)

(11) Revolving mixer arms in casings.
   (Dough mixers; rubber solution mixers; and the like.)

(12) Revolving worms and spirals in casings.
   (Meat mincers; rubber extruders; spiral conveyors; and the like.)

(13) Revolving high-speed cages in casings.
   (Hydro-extractors; centrifuges; and the like.)

(14) Revolving cutting tools.
>   (Circular saws; milling cutters; circular shears; wood slicers; chaff cutters; and the like.)

(15) Reciprocating tools and dies.
>   (Power presses; drop stamps; relief stamping presses; hydraulic and pneumatic presses; bending brakes; revolution presses; and others.)

(16) Reciprocating knives and saws.
>   (Guillotines: metal-, rubber-, and paper-cutting; trimmers; perforators; and the like.)

(17) Platen motions.
>   (Letterpress printing machines; paper and cardboard cutters; and similar adaptations.)

(18) Projecting belt fasteners and fast-running belts.
>   (Bolt and nut fasteners; wire pin fasteners; and the like; woodworking machinery belts; centrifuge belts; textile machinery side belting; and others.)

(19) Pawl and notched wheel devices for intermittent feed motions.
>   (Planer tool feed motions; power press dial feed tables; and the like.)

(20) Abrasive wheels.
>   (Manufactured wheels; natural sandstones; and others.)

(21) Moving balance weights and deadweights.
>   (Hydraulic accumulators; counterbalance weights on large slotting machines; and others.)

(22) Nips between travelling and fixed parts.
>   (Travelling conveyor hoppers and tipping cams, bars or other fixed parts; inclined bucket conveyor and fixed parts; and the like.)

Safety of the Place of Work Excluding Plant and Machinery

There is almost as much case law on this topic as there is on the fencing sections, but it is not nearly so well known; possibly because it is less exciting. Certainly it is just as important. There are many sections which deal with general safety of the workplace. Some of them such as ss. 5 (lighting)

and 6 (drainage of floors) masquerade as "health" provisions
though their primary importance is clearly one of safety.
Others such as s. 18 (fencing of vessels containing dangerous
substances) are reasonably straightforward and are accessible
to a careful reading. The massive and important provisions
of ss. 40–52 regarding fire precautions are tedious but straightforward; they need no gloss to be understood.

Sections 28 and 29 which deal with "floors, passages and
stairs" and "safe means of access and safe place of employment" respectively are a different matter. Not merely are they
of great practical importance (over 20 per cent of all serious
accidents are caused by hazards dealt with by these two sections) but they have been the subject of considerable judicial
interpretation.

Section 28 requires, amongst other less important things,
that:

> "All floors, steps, stairs, passages and gangways shall be
> of sound construction and properly maintained and shall,
> so far as is reasonably practicable, be kept free from any
> obstruction and from any substance likely to cause per-
> sons to slip."

The requirements as to "sound construction" and "properly
maintained" are straightforward. They refer to the basic construction and suitability of the floors, steps, etc., and to their
maintenance after construction. The requirement is "absolute"; if any of these things collapse the occupier is liable.

"Obstruction" means something that should not be there
in the normal decent course of working. The proper storage
of things on the floor is all right. So is the temporary presence
of a trolly in the ordinary course of work. What is "reasonably
practicable" is a source of trouble:

> A workman was seriously injured when he fell over help-
> ing to carry a casting in a foundry. He tripped over a
> "gate": part of a casting which is knocked off when the
> casting is completed. The gate was hidden in the sand
> in the knocking-out area. This area was cleaned of gates
> and sand every day. The House of Lords held (i) by

a majority, that the gate was an "obstruction" within the
meaning of s. 28, and (ii) that it was not reasonably practicable to keep the floor free from such "obstructions".
They appear to have been much influenced by the fact
that the injured man himself (who was very experienced)
and his foreman were unable to suggest a method by
which the floor could be kept free.

Jenkins v. *Allied Ironfounders Ltd* (1969) HL

In the case of substances "likely to cause persons to slip"
the courts have tended to ignore trivial faults or defects on
the basis that it is impracticable to avoid them.

Section 29 (1) is much more general:

"There shall, so far as is reasonably practicable, be provided and maintained safe means of access to every place
at which any person has at any time to work, and every
such place shall, so far as is reasonably practicable, be
made and kept safe for any person working there."

Almost every word of this subsection needs careful consideration:

Means of access

The means of access have to be distinguished from the place
of work; the standards prescribed by the section for the two
are different. The section covers every possible kind of means
of access: gangways, ladders, crawling boards, roofs, etc. Anything that the workman *uses* as a means of access *is* one for
the purposes of the section. But if the workman uses an
unsafe means when a safe means has been provided, the occupier is under no liability unless the unsafe means has been
offered *by him* as an alternative or *accepted* by him (or by
someone acting on his behalf, *e.g.* a foreman) as an alternative.

The means of access must be structurally sound though,
as in the case of s. 28 above, transient defects arising out
of normal use will not be regarded as being in breach of the
section.

A means of access may also be a *place of work*. In which

case "it is necessary to see for which purpose it is being used, or may require to be used, at the material time" in order to decide which standard applies (Devlin, J., in *Dorman Long Ltd.* v. *Hillier* (1951) DC).

The means of access must be to a place of work. The access to a canteen or a lavatory does not come within the section. If the means of access is used for more than one purpose, *i.e.* to get to a lavatory *and* to get to a place of work, then, if injury occurs when it is being used, liability depends upon which of the purposes it was being used for at the time. If it was to get to the place of work then there is a breach.

Provided

The meaning of this word is by no means clear:

> A workman was seriously injured when he climbed up some temporary scaffolding. Ladders were "available" in the stores some little distance away and he knew this. It was held that safe means of access had been "provided" and that there was no breach of the section.

> *Farquar* v. *Chance Bros. Ltd.* (1951) DC

Contrast:

> A workman received an injury to an eye whilst grinding. He was not wearing goggles. They were required to be "provided" under s. 49 of the Act of 1937. There were plenty of goggles in the foreman's office, but the man had not been told where they were kept. The rule was that he had to ask for them when he wanted them. The court held that the goggles were not "provided".

> *Finch* v. *Telegraph Construction & Maintenance Co. Ltd.* (1949) KBD

The distinction between these two cases appears to be the information given to the workman. If they are kept properly informed it is believed that *Farquar's* case represents the true legal position.

Place

When, as is so often the case, the person involved is working from a ladder, the "place" of work is the ladder; not the area in which the ladder is being used.

Section 29(2) provides:

"Where any person has to work at a place from which he will be liable to fall a distance of more than six feet six inches, then, unless the place is one which affords secure foothold and, where necessary, secure handhold, means shall be provided, so far as is reasonably practicable, by fencing or otherwise, for ensuring his safety."

Again it needs almost word-for-word consideration:

Any person

This certainly includes servants of independent contractors who are working in the factory. It will not include persons "casually" in the factory:

"The real question is what is meant by the words 'any person' . . . They cannot be of entirely general application: I agree that a policeman who enters a factory in pursuit of a felon, or a fireman who enters to put out a fire, is not within the section, although he is a 'person' and he is 'working' . . . In my view, the true distinction is between those who are to work for the purposes of the factory and those who are not" (Viscount Kilmuir in *Wigley* v. *British Vinegars* (1962) HL).

Liable to fall

There is no authority for the proposition, but it is suggested that the "liability" must be assessed objectively. That is, the personal peculiarities of the workman are irrelevant. So, if the workman has a wooden leg or suffers from epilepsy this does *not* make him any more "liable to fall" within the meaning of the section. (Though these personal peculiarities may affect the employer's common law liabilities. See p. 129.)

The work that the workman is doing will, however, affect his liability to fall.

Secure foothold . . . secure handhold

The handhold or foothold is "secure" if it is adequate for a workman acting in a way he might reasonably be expected to act in circumstances that might reasonably be expected to occur. If he is working from a ladder the upright of the ladder is normally a secure handhold *provided the workman can use it* (*Wigley* v. *British Vinegars Ltd.* (1961) HL). It would seem impossible that work from a ladder can comply with the sub-section if it requires the continual use of both hands.

> A workman was blown from his place of work when there was an explosion in the factory. There was no breach of the section as the foothold provided was adequate for all reasonably foreseeable circumstances.
>
> *Tinto* v. *Stewart & Lloyds Ltd.* (1962) QBD

Some Aspects of Health and Welfare Provisions

The majority of health and welfare provisions are simple enough to be assimilated direct from the Act. There are a few, however, which present problems of interpretation and application. The most interesting and important are as follows:

Washing Facilities (s. 58)

"Adequate and suitable" washing facilities must be provided. To be "adequate and suitable" the facilities must include running hot and cold or warm water; there must also be towels or other suitable means of cleaning or drying.

The section also gives the Minister power to make regulations creating a "standard of adequate and suitable washing facilities". So far the only regulations made have provided for exemption at the discretion of the district inspector. However, many other codes of regulations do contain specific provisions as to washing facilities, *e.g.* the Iron and Steel Foundries Regulations 1953. It is, therefore, necessary to check whether any regulations have been made in respect of any particular trade.

In the absence of any regulations, the key words of the section are "adequate and suitable". Unfortunately they have seldom been considered by the superior courts. They probably mean that the washing facilities must be adequate and suitable (i) in relation to the numbers of people involved, and (ii) in relation to the kind of work that is being done. So, it is suggested, the facilities can only be adequate and suitable in the case of dirty jobs which involve dirtying the whole body when facilities are provided for cleansing the whole body, *i.e.* baths or showers.

It has been held that this section can give rise to action for breach of statutory duty if it can be shown that the failure to supply adequate and suitable washing facilities caused the injury (*e.g.* dermatitis cases). The problems of proof are such that it is hard to believe that this right will ever be important.

Finally, although this section comes in Part III of the Act which is described as "Welfare (General Provisions)" it is hard to believe (especially in the light of the comment above on the question of breach of statutory duty) that it is not also a "health" provision by any realistic assessment. If this is so then the employee is bound, by the provisions of s. 143(1) (see p. 174) to make use of the washing facilities and can be prosecuted if he does not. No such prosecution has ever been taken.

Accommodation for Clothing (s. 59)

As in the case of washing facilities the standard prescribed for accommodation for clothing is that it should be "adequate and suitable". Precisely the same considerations apply in interpreting this phrase as did in the earlier section. It would not have been worth considering the section at all were it not for the odd little case of *McCarthy* v. *Daily Mirror Newspapers Ltd.* (1949) CA:

> The plaintiff claimed damages from his employer for the loss of clothing from a peg provided for his use whilst at work. He based his claim partly on breach of statutory duty: that the accommodation was not "adequate and suitable". The County Court judge rejected the claim. The Court of Appeal remitted the case back to the

County Court with instructions to the judge to consider the possibility of theft in relation to the adequacy and suitability of the accommodation.

It seems clear from this case that, whilst the theft of clothing does not necessarily mean a breach of the section, the possibility of theft is something that has to be considered when making arrangements to comply with it.

Dust and Fumes (ss. 1, 4, 63 and 30)

Section 1 has only a marginal application to this topic. It does, however, require the daily removal of "dirt and refuse", and dust comes into this category.

Section 4(1), though badly drafted, requires the removal of "fumes, dust and other impurities generated in the course of any process or work carried on in the factory as may be injurious to health". This removal is to be done by the "circulation of fresh air" and "adequate ventilation", and is limited to "practicable" means. This section should be contrasted with s. 63 (dealt with below) which deals primarily with preventing the "impurities" getting into the air of the workroom. Section 4 starts where s. 63 leaves off: when the "impurities" are in the air. The liability imposed by s. 4 is not "absolute" in that the efforts made have to be "practicable". This is a higher standard than "reasonably practicable", but the fact that any qualification is used at all limits its effect to some extent:

> ". . . in my judgement, there may well be precautions which it is 'practicable' but not 'reasonably practicable' to take . . . I think it enough to say that, if a precaution is practicable it must be taken unless, in the whole circumstances, that would be unreasonable. As men's lives may be at stake it should not lightly be held that to take a practicable precaution is unreasonable" (Lord Reid in *Marshall* v. *Gotham Co. Ltd* (1954) HL).

The onus of showing that something is "impracticable" under the section falls on the occupier.

There is some dispute as to whether the occupier of the factory needs to *know* of the existence of the "impurities" before his obligation to get rid of them begins. (Or, of course, *ought* to have known about them as a reasonable employer.) There are some indications in the judgement of the Court of Appeal in the case of *Ebbs* v. *James Whitson & Co. Ltd.* (1952) CA that the words of the section are to be construed literally and that "impurities" must be removed by "practicable" means whether the occupier knows of them or not. Although there are dicta to the contrary it seems likely that this view is correct. The limitation placed on the "absoluteness" of the obligation by the use of the word "practicable" is, therefore, limited to the means used.

It appears that this is one of the borderline sections which may give rise to an action for breach of statutory duty as well as liability to prosecution.

As pointed out above, s. 4 begins where s. 63 leaves off. The latter imposes two distinct duties:

First, where any process gives off "any dust or fume or other impurity of such a character and to such an extent as to be likely to be injurious or offensive to the persons employed", then "all practicable measures" must be taken to prevent persons inhaling the impurity, to prevent its accumulation in a workroom and, "where the nature of the process makes it practicable", exhaust ventilation appliances must be used at the source.

Second, where a process creates "any substantial quantity of dust *of any kind*" (*i.e.* whether harmful or not) the same precautions must be taken.

There are, of course, the same problems over the meaning of the word "practicable" as those discussed above and the same principles apply. More difficult are the words "likely to be injurious or offensive". This terminology is, either by accident or design, quite different from that used in s. 4(1) ". . . all such . . . impurities . . . as may be injurious to health." It would seem that the words used in s. 63 are less mandatory than those of s. 4(1) and that their result is not so "absolute":

> "It seems to me to be fully arguable that this section is primarily, if not wholly, directed to measures of preventing the inhalation of dust, and further, that the mea-

sures are only required to be taken when . . . there is given off either (i) a dust which is likely to be injurious or offensive to the persons employed in the factory in the sense of likely to be injurious *according to the estimation of a reasonably well-informed factory occupier* or which the actual occupier knew, or ought to have known, to be likely to be injurious or (ii) dust present, of any kind, in substantial quantities" (McNair, J., in *Ebbs* v. *James Whitson & Co. Ltd.* (1952) QBD; the italics are added).

The standard required by the first duty of s. 63 is, therefore, lower than that of s. 4(1).

Perhaps a little oddly, the second duty, to control "any substantial quantity of dust [of any kind]", *is* phrased in "absolute" terms. As in the case of s. 4(1) the "absoluteness" of the requirement is mitigated by the fact that the *means used* need only be such as are "practicable".

Section 30, though much longer than either s. 4 or s. 63, presents no difficulties of interpretation. It deals with entering enclosed spaces where there may be dangerous fumes and/or lack of oxygen and lays down an elaborate procedure to be followed. There is no authority on the point, but it is at least strongly arguable that the word "certified" in sub-ss. 4 and 5 implies a written certificate.

Lifting Excessive Weights (s. 72)

Over 70,000 reportable accidents in factories in 1972 were sustained by persons "handling goods". This is about 20 per cent of all reportable accidents. (For the meaning of "reportable accident" see p. 169.) It is, therefore, perhaps a little surprising that the only section of the Act which deals with the manual handling of goods and materials is s. 72 (though the Pottery (Health and Welfare) Regulations contains some specific provisions on lifting heavy weights). The section provides:

> "A person shall not be employed to lift, carry or move any load so heavy as to be likely to cause injury to him."

Subsection (2) of the section gives the Minister power to make regulations on the subject, but none have as yet been made.

This rather feeble section has been killed by judicial interpretation. In *Kinsella* v. *Harris Lebus* (1963) the Court of
Appeal held that a weight of 145 lbs. was not "likely to cause
injury" to an experienced worker and that employment to lift
such a weight was not in breach of the section. In a second
recent case:

> P was employed by the defendants to do a job which
> involved lifting lengths of chain about 65 lbs. weight a
> height of about 18″. P had only one leg and a record
> of back trouble: all known to his employers. He was one
> of a gang of four men (all physically handicapped) and
> his foreman had told him to ask other members of the
> gang for help if he felt he needed it. P hurt his back
> seriously when lifting a length of chain. The Court of
> Appeal held that there was no breach of the section.

Peat v. *N. J. Muschamp & Co. Ltd.* (1969) CA

Taken together these two cases mean:

(i) The section is useless as a criminal provision. The
use of the word "employed" instead of some such
word as "allowed" has resulted in a narrow construction which is fatal.

(ii) In civil cases an action is hopeless if help is available.

Regulations

As was pointed out earlier, the dominant pattern of the Factories Act is: general provision followed sometimes by more
detailed requirements on the same topic; followed, in turn, by
power given to the Minister to make regulations or orders.
So, s. 1 starts off with the classic proposition: "Every factory
shall be kept in a clean state . . ." Subsections 2 and 3 then
go on to elaborate on this theme "without prejudice to the
generality" of the initial requirement. Subsection 4 allows the
District Inspector of Factories some powers of exemption from
specific requirements and, finally, subsection 5 gives the
Minister powers to make supplementary provisions, in this
case by Ministerial order rather than by regulations. This pat-

tern, save that the Ministerial power is more usually to make regulations, is repeated again and again throughout the Act.

In addition to powers to make regulations on specific topics, two sections give the Minister more general powers. Section 62 deals with welfare matters; s. 76 safety and health. About 130 sets of regulations are now in force. All are concerned with *processes* and apply to factories in which the regulated process is being carried on. For example, the Aerated Water Regulations 1921 apply "to all factories . . . or parts thereof in which is carried on the manufacture of aerated water and processes incidental thereto."

The manner of making regulations is laid down in s. 180. There are provisions in the fourth schedule for the holding of public enquiries in the case of objections to draft regulations which have to be published in the *London Gazette*. After the regulations have been laid before Parliament either House can annul them within 40 days. After the 40 days they have the force of statute.

It is important to understand the relationship between regulations and the Act proper. The Minister's powers are very wide. In general he can:

(i) *Make regulations about hazards that the Act had never contemplated*

The Act of 1961 is effectively still the 1937 Act with minor modifications. Hazards from radioactivity in industry were unthought of at that time. The dangers from the contemporary use of isotopes have been dealt with by a series of regulations made under s. 76.

(ii) *Mitigate the provisions of the Act*

The application of s. 14(1) of the Act would mean that a woodworking circular saw could not legally be used. The only way of fencing it securely would be complete enclosure of the blade (cf. *John Summers & Sons Ltd.* v. *Frost*, p. 182). This dilemma is resolved by regulation 10 of the Woodworking Machinery Regulations 1922 which provides for a *lesser* standard of fencing for the blade and is *in substitution for* the requirements of s. 14(1).

(iii) *Make the requirements of the Act more stringent*

The fencing of the trap between the tool and die of a power-press is dealt with by s. 14(1). It has to be "securely fenced". The Power Presses Regulations 1965 impose many additional responsibilities in respect of examination, testing and records. Regulation 3(3) stipulates that the regulations "are in addition to and not in substitution for or in diminution of other requirements imposed by or under the principal Act".

This last provision is important. Where regulations deal with a particular hazard they will be regarded as being in substitution for the relevant requirements of the Act (if any) unless otherwise provided:

> The Grinding of Metals (Miscellaneous Industries) Regulations 1925 dealt with the same subject-matter as s. 47 of the Act of 1937 (now s. 63 of the 1961 Act, see p. 196). The Court of Appeal held that the regulations were in substitution of the requirements of the section which was, therefore, inoperative (*Franklin* v. *Gramophone Co. Ltd.* (1948) CA). It should be noted that the regulations were amended to make them additional to, and not in substitution for, the requirements of the Act.

On the other hand, the fact that regulations deal specifically with one dangerous part of a machine does not exclude the application of the Act to other parts of the same machine:

> Regulation 3 of the Horizontal Milling Machines Regulations 1928 lays down special rules for the fencing of the cutters of such machines. The standard prescribed is higher than that of s. 14(1) of the Act. A workman was hurt on another part of the machine. The Court held that the Act applied to all other dangerous parts of the machine even though regulation 3 applied to the cutter and was exhaustive so far as that part was concerned.

Benn v. *Kamm & Co. Ltd.* (1952) CA

"Notional" Factories

Sections 123–127 extend the operation of the Act, or parts of it, to premises and activities that would, otherwise, be excluded. Electrical stations (s. 123), charitable and reformatory institutions (a somewhat blood-curdling coupling in s. 124), docks, wharves, quays and warehouses (s. 125), ships (s. 126) and building operations and works of engineering construction (s. 127) all become, to a greater or lesser extent, subject to the Act. The provisions of the Act that apply to each can readily be found out by reference to the appropriate section. There are no problems of interpretation. Thus, they all become "factories" for certain purposes.

The most important result of these sections is that the Minister has power to make regulations relating to work done in these places. Many of these regulations provide elaborate codes of practice almost as compendious as the Act itself.

As these places become "factories" for the purposes of the Act the occupiers become liable to inspection and prosecution in precisely the same way as the occupiers of a conventional factory.

VII   THE OFFICES, SHOPS AND RAILWAY PREMISES ACT 1963

In addition to the Factories Acts, many other specialised types of employment are subject to statutory control. Most of the other statutes such as those relating to mines and quarries and nuclear installations are too esoteric for a book of this kind, but the legislation relating to offices, shops and railway premises is potentially so far-reaching that it must be dealt with, albeit briefly.

Broadly speaking, the Act is based on the factories legislation, though rather heavier emphasis is placed upon the use of regulations. Unfortunately the implementation of the Act has been left in the hands of local authorities (with limited exceptions) and the degree of enforcement is, therefore, highly suspect. If a highly skilled and experienced body such as the Factory Inspectorate cannot cope with their obligations (see p. 171) it is clearly likely that local councils will be unable to do even as well with the multitudinous premises that come within the scope of the Act. This is, perhaps, reflected in the virtual absence of case law on the statute. Possibly the only part of the Act which has become meaningful is that concerned with fire precautions. This has been placed in the hands of fire authorities, who are notoriously efficient however small or understaffed.

Premises Covered by the Act

As in the Factories Act, the premises are defined largely by activity. "Office processes" (not a term used in the Act but used here by analogy with "factory process", see p. 166) are not exhaustively defined, but s. 1 sets out activities that do come within the scope of the Act. This type of "inclusive" but not exhaustive definition is to be deprecated but is all too common in English statutes.

In addition to straight office activities, premises used in conjunction with those in which office activities are carried on are covered.

Limitations are imposed. Personal dwelling houses are excluded as are premises in which only close relatives are employed (s. 2).

Finally, there must be a minimum of 21 hours a week office activity for the Act to apply.

Safety

The safety provisions are so closely modelled on those of the parent Act as to need little comment. Similar terminology, such as the use of the word "dangerous", implies identical interpretation. The main variation in form from that of the Factories Act is that the classification of machinery into prime movers, transmission machinery and "other dangerous parts" (see p. 178) has very sensibly been abandoned. Section 17 simply provides that any dangerous part of any machinery used as equipment in the premises be securely fenced.

Another interesting innovation is that s. 21 gives the Secretary of State the power to make regulations in respect of noise or vibrations which might cause injury or damage to the health of employed persons. No such regulations have as yet been made.

Health and Welfare

Once again the pattern of the Factories Act is perpetuated: general provision coupled with the power to make regulations. The scope of the Act is almost identical with that of the Factories Act, though there are differences of detail.

Fire

The most important single provision is that any premises in which more than 20 persons work or more than 10 persons are employed on other than a ground floor, or where highly inflammable or explosive materials are stored, must have a fire certificate granted by the fire authority (s. 29). Such a certificate will not, of course, be granted unless the authority is satisfied as to the safety of the premises. There is also power (s. 32) for a magistrate to make an order prohibiting the use of a building or part of it on the grounds of fire-hazard (cf. Factories Act provisions, p. 171).

Conclusions

The potential of the Act is considerable. It is not believed that it is being realised. Probably its main use at the moment is that it may give an action for breach of statutory duty (see p. 131) to employees who have previously not had one.

Index

205

Index

STATE OF EMERGENCY
declaration of, 6, 118
limitations on, 118–119

STATUTORY DUTY
breach of, action for, 131–132
protective statutes, 132–135

STRIKE. *See also* INDUSTRIAL ACTION;
LOCK-OUT
ballot, conduct of, 120
order, issue of, 120
definition, 116

TERMS AND CONDITIONS OF
EMPLOYMENT ACT 1959
amended by Industrial Relations Act, 18
compulsory arbitration under, 18

TORTS, 109–113
breach of contract, inducement of,
110–112
conspiracy, 109–110
intimidation as, 112
negligence as, 121

TRADE UNION
bargaining, independent agent during, 94
definition—
Act of 1971 in, 70
Code of Practice in, 70
de-registration, method, 71
funds protected from claims for damages,
114
history, 68
industrial disputes, immunity in, 113
legalised by Trade Union Act 1871, 68
membership, 7
discipline of, 90
rights, 77
right to hold, 90
resign, 89
termination of, 90
objects of, under 1971 Act, 70
offices, right to hold, 89
political activities, legalised, 74
fund—
contributions to, 74–75
establishment, 74
registered—
application of 1913 Act to, 74
approved closed shop application, 83
conduct, guiding principles of, 89–90
legal persons as, 73
limited liability in respect of awards of
compensation by NIRC, 118
options open to, 7
participation in activities at work, 78
position under 1971 Act, 69

TRADE UNION—*continued*
registered—*continued*
records, 73–74
Registrar, subject to authority of, 71
rules for, listed, 72
alteration of, 72
breach of, 73
winding-up, 74
registration—
method of, 70–71
under Trade Union Act 1871, 68
rule book—
compliance with Industrial Relations
Act, 71
examination of, 71
unregistered—
application of 1913 Act to, 74
conduct, guiding principles of, 89–90
position under 1971 Act, 69
vote, right to, 89

TRADE UNION ACT 1913
application to—
registered unions, 74
unregistered unions, 74
political activities legalised by, 74

TRADE UNION CONGRESS
policy towards registration, 70

TRUCK PAYMENTS. *See also* WAGES
fines as, 38
national insurance contributions, 58
prohibition of, 31

UNDERTAKING, 7. *See also* UNIT OF
EMPLOYMENT; BARGAINING UNIT

UNEMPLOYMENT BENEFIT. *See also*
BENEFITS; NATIONAL INSURANCE
grounds for, 59
strikers, not entitled to, 60

UNFAIR DISMISSAL, 5, 7
appeals against, 48
compensation for, 48
crown servants may appeal against, 48
Industrial Relations Act, under, 48
Industrial Tribunals, consideration by,
48, 49
re-instatement of employee, 55

UNFAIR INDUSTRIAL PRACTICE
blacking, 115
breach of collective agreement, 95, 115
guiding principles, 91
definition, 115
inducement to breach of contract, 111
interference with agency shop ballot, 83
negotiations other than with sole
bargaining agency, 101